I0187133

THE BREEDING
OF CONTEMPT
By
John W. King
2nd Edition

<u>CONTENTS</u>

Dedication Page

This book is dedicated to the memories of the precious lives lost in the Khaalis home on January 18, 1973. You are important martyrs in our human struggle towards truth, and you will never be forgotten.

Abdullah Khaalis

Abdul Tasibur Khaalis

Bibi Khaalis

Daud Khaalis

Khadyja Khaalis

Rahman Uddein Khaalis

Adul Nur

ACKNOWLEDGMENTS

I wish to give acknowledgements to those people who not only understood my need to write and publish this book, but who also gave much love and support to me in the process. First and foremost, my mother, Jeanette, who realized that her life would be exposed in telling this story, but gave me all of her love and support. Thanks, Mom, I love you too. Second, my siblings who endured this with me, thank you Dana, Darshell, Quram. I love you all; thanks for understanding my need to record this part of our family history. Dana, thank you forever for being the first reader of the piece. Thanks so much to my editor, Connie Thompson. Connie, without you I could have never revised this book, you've been a driving force and great motivation for me. Amelia Mraz, who did a great deal of typing, as well as adding great ideas such as the timeline, Thank you for your invaluable contributions Amelia. Finally, I'd like to thank my daughter Asha, and my granddaughter Aasiya, who remind me of why I needed to continue to tell this story, as I am so very grateful for their lives.

FOREWARD

When I initially wrote this narrative more than twenty years ago, and published in 2003, not only did I not realize what I didn't know about some of the people I wrote about, I also had no idea of the positive response I would receive from its arrival. At the heart of this story are the Khaalis children who lost their lives in 1973, that is an uncompromising arch of this story which I hope will remain in the minds of readers as they navigate their way through this very complex narrative. Since the arrival of this book, and the subsequent documentary (American Gangster: Philly Black Mafia), I received a variety of offers to further share the story on screen, in university auditoriums as well as on street corners. The response has been overwhelming, but at the same time has left me with a feeling of incompleteness. The feeling of incompleteness comes from two places, first it comes from the fact that I initially relied on my own personal memories of conversations I had been privy to either being in or overhearing by sheer happenstance.

It also came from my own youthful impatience to finish the book, knowing that I didn't necessarily have the full account of certain individuals deemed important to the narrative. I was Thirty-Two when I began to seriously write The Breeding of Contempt, and if I'm being honest, part of my motivation at that time was to cathartically provide some relief to my own pain of loss. I lost my paternal grandmother, my father's only brother and my maternal grandfather all within a six week period that year, and so the writing was initially for my own benefit. Once I got past the first one hundred pages, I came to realize the narrative was much greater than my own pain.

Since the publishing and documentary, I have had the opportunity to befriend Eugene "Bo" Baynes, Sam Christian, Donny Day, Ronald Harvey Jr., and Rhonda Coxsom, the only child of Major Coxson. I also received a wonderful letter from a family member of the Khaalis, who freed me of my own pain and guilt of association with their very poignant letter, recognizing my pain and need for reconciliation. Of course, I had a familiarity with Sam Chrisitian and Bo Baynes, as they were not only acquaintances of my father, but they were legends in Black Philadelphia underworld communities. During the early 2000's Bo (or Abu, as most called him) owned several restaurants in Philadelphia, upon his release from federal prison in 1991, most notably "The Garden of Bilal" in the Mount Airy section of Philadelphia. So on occasion, I would visit the restaurant to hear great live jazz performances, but also enjoy the food and catch a glimpse of the legend himself. Once Bo realized whose son I was, he literally rolled out the red carpet of welcome, and provided me full access to himself. Bo was never one to sit around telling stories about others' cases or give explanations on why things went south for the organization, but he provided me with insights and motivations that I wished I had prior to writing the book.

Equally so, Sam Christian (whom most of us referred to as Beyat) was very welcoming to me. I often served as his de facto driver when he visited Philadelphia from Detroit (where he had been living since his release from prison in 1988). Sam's sister was sick, I believe from cancer, and on occasion he would come for a visit, but didn't want to alert some elements (be they law enforcement or others) that he was in town. So on those rare occasions, I would meet Sam at the bus station and we'd drive to South Philly. Both Bo and Sam thoroughly understood the value of their nefarious contributions to the Philadelphia underworld, and were interested in having the story told. Bo actually participated in the documentary with me, and subsequently facilitated a summit at his home to strategize our movements around the story.

As my interests were solely about the deaths of the Khaalis family, and the survival of my own family while in the federal witness protection program, my motivation was a bit myopic. Though I must admit, I was honored to be present for the meeting. Sam couldn't make it at the time, but sent a representative to express his interest. Sham Su-din Ali (then the lead Imam for the muslim population in Philadelphia, prior to his conviction on charges of fraud) also sent a representative, his nephew. Donnie Day, one of the known founders of the Black Mafia in Philadelphia was present and equally interested in the conversation.

This was the first and last time I met and got to speak with Donnie Day, who was elated to meet me. Donnie felt a bit out of his element as the remaining years hadn't been so good to him. He had a bout of heroin addiction and was deemed unreliable to some even during the mafia's heyday because of his weakness to the substance. As honored as I was to be present, as a writer I had a desire to continue to seek the truth about some of the dramatic events most people in the room simply weren't talking about. I found that opportunity in Donnie Day. Craving a cigarette, and the need to remove himself from the opulent furnishings of Bo's lavish home, I invited Donnie Day to step out on the front porch for a smoke, even though I didn't smoke. I sensed Donnie could use an audience of one to tell his story, as the inside conversation was being led by Bo. I was surprised how freely Donnie spoke about the organization, and I couldn't resist asking him about the main incident that alluded me for years, the murder of Major Coxson. In the chapter titled "The Maje," you will not only hear my voice but Donnie Day's remembrance of what occurred and why it occurred, and even more important, you'll hear from Major Coxson's daughter, Rhonda, whom I met by pure happenstance some years later.

I must say, I am grateful to have met and known Sam Christian, Bo Baynes and Donnie Day, all of whom have since passed away. I am equally grateful to have met both Ronald Harvey Jr. and Rhonda Coxsom, whom I call my friends. I honestly had zero intention of writing a second edition to The Breeding of Contempt, but the universe clearly had other ideas. As someone in their early fifties now, with a greater understanding of the tragedies and how they are all connected to one another, I feel very grateful for the divine intervention and I hope this second edition provides you with a better understanding of how young men from disenfranchised communities made choices that brought these incidents into being and indirectly gave birth to my own misunderstandings and pathology, leading to a reconciliation of my own perceptions of our humanity. I hope you enjoy, and more importantly understand The Breeding of Contempt, 2nd edition.

CHAPTER ONE

The Massacre

There were major events occurring in the nation's capital on Wednesday, January 17, 1973. The city was preparing to inaugurate Richard M. Nixon for his second term as president, just as the investigation into the Watergate break-in began to inch closer and closer to the White House. All of the political insiders were in Washington that week, as well as all of the media organizations to cover the Presidential Inauguration. Due to the presidential events, all of the major hotels in the city were fully occupied, as well as most of the motels.

At 9:30 p.m. on Wednesday, January 17th two cars full of young black men pulled up to a downtown motel at 501 New York Avenue, located in the Northeast section of Washington. One of the cars was a late model Cadillac Sedan Deville, the other a late model Chrysler. The motel clerk watched from the window as the cars pulled up to the lot. She wondered to herself whether the black men were here for the President's inauguration, but she dismissed that as a possibility because the president was Republican and very unpopular with the majority of black groups. Then, she thought maybe they're here to demonstrate against the president while he's being inaugurated.

As she finished her thought, two men got out of the late model Cadillac, as the others sat in the cars waiting. The two men were about six feet tall, one had a light complexion, and the other was darker. Both men had on very expensive suits, which changed the clerk's opinion that maybe the men were southern freedom riders or clergy. These men were from a big city, possibly in the northeast.

The light skinned man walked up to the desk as the dark skinned man waited about two feet behind. The light skinned man asked the clerk if there were any rooms available. The clerk responded, "Yes, we have only two rooms left." The light skinned man expressed a sigh of relief. He said, "Great! We'll take them both. We've been to three motels already, and they all were filled to capacity." The clerk asked suspiciously, "You gentleman in town for the Inauguration?" The light skinned man responded quickly, "No, just doing a little sightseeing." The rapid response was an indication to the clerk that the men were not interested in playing Twenty Questions, so she handed the light skinned man a registration card. The light skinned man filled out the card signing a party of six, and signed the card William Horton.

The clerk had a full view of the two cars, and she could clearly see that there was one man left in the late model Cadillac, and four men sitting in the late model Chrysler. With the two men standing in front of her, the total was seven. She then asked if all the men in both cars were going to stay in the motel. The dark skinned man, who was standing two feet behind "Mr. Horton" replied, "They're all staying except for me." The clerk thought to herself, why then would this man accompany Mr. Horton to the office to register if he was not staying? Was he a bodyguard? Were they a group of performers reduced to using the motel because of the inauguration, or were they just trying to get away without paying the $5.00 per person surcharge on the rooms when there are more than three people occupying? Whichever it was, the clerk didn't pursue the matter any further.

She gave "Mr. Horton" the keys for both rooms; he thanked her and left the office. "Mr. Horton," the dark skinned man, and the one remaining in the Cadillac took room 27, and the four men from the Chrysler took room 29 in the motel.

At 10:15 p.m. the four men from room 29 joined their friends in room 27 for a meeting. They met to discuss their reasons for coming to Washington D.C. Before the meeting, the dark skinned man laughed as he thought about the clerk's probing questions. He said to the others, "She probably thought we were some kind of rabble rousers coming to bother Nixon."

These men were not in town for the inauguration, nor to protest against the Vietnam War. In their meeting, there was a discussion about the murder of a leader, but it was not the President. Mr. Horton had gathered his associates for a short meeting to discuss how they were going to carry out the assassination of the man they referred to simply as "the leader."

Mr. Horton told the others he had come down to Washington only yesterday to see "the leader's" house for himself, but he wanted everyone to see it so that they could decide on the escape routes. All the men agreed. So Mr. Horton, the dark skinned man, and two of the four men from room 29 decided to go to "the leader's" house that evening in hopes of securing escape routes.

At 10:45 p.m. the four men drove to the Northwest section Washington to take a look at the exits while the three remaining waited at the motel. At approximately 11:00 p.m. a caller from out of town phoned into the motel. The call was transferred to room 27 where the three men remained after their meeting. The call was from an eighth associate, the actual owner of the late model Cadillac. The eighth associate called to see how things were progressing, and also to give the arrival time of his train into Washington on the next day.

At 11:45 p.m. the four men returned. Since it was late, Mr. Horton decided that they would give out the information on escape routes in the morning. They all retired to their rooms.

At approximately 8:30 a.m. on Thursday, January 18, 1973, the four men from room 29 returned once again to room 27 for a meeting. Mr. Horton led the meeting with a morning prayer then he stated the schedule for the day. Mr. Horton told his associates that the three who stayed behind last night would have an opportunity to see the house this morning to get a view of the escape routes. He also said that they had agreed upon three escape routes that would be taken when they checked out the house the previous evening, but he wanted the remaining three to see if they agreed with the routes. The three associates left directly after the meeting to check out the premises. They returned a little after 10:00 a.m. that morning.

At 10:30 all seven men went to breakfast in downtown Washington. At breakfast Mr. Horton made a call on the pay phone to "the leader's" home. A man answered, and Mr. Horton asked if they needed any work done on the premise; he said he was a handyman looking for work. Mr. Horton added that a friend had mentioned to him that they were looking for a handyman. The man responded that they were looking for someone to fix the locks on their basement door. He told Mr. Horton to come around noon. About five minutes later another associate made a second call to the house and the same man answered. This time, the associate told the man that he had heard great things about his organization, and that he wanted to purchase books if they had any available. The man responded, "Yes, we do. Why don't you come here today, and we will sell you a few pamphlets."

The seven associates had finished their breakfast, and were now sitting contently with their plan in motion. At 11:00 a.m. the men piled into the two cars, and drove to Washington's train station. At 11:15 a.m. they picked up their eighth associate and returned to their motel rooms for one final meeting. At 12:05 p.m., another clerk on duty noticed eight black men leaving room 27. She said, "Four men got into a gray Cadillac, and the other four got into a yellow Chrysler."

At 12:30 p.m. that afternoon, the eight men successfully reached their destination, the house at 7700 16th Street, NW Washington, D.C. The two cars parked a block away from the intended house. The first to get out of the vehicles were the two youngest of the eight men entourage. They got out of the Chrysler and walked up to the house.

Along with being the youngest, they were also the shortest. Both stood about five feet and a half feet tall. They were both dressed well wearing full length wool Chesterfield coats, with black leather gloves. Their impeccably well-dressed appearances were thrown off balance due to the single cigarettes that lay behind their right ears.

They rung the bell, and a young man wearing religious garments answered the door. The two young men then greeted the man and said that they had phoned earlier about purchasing some pamphlets about his organization. The young man, who answered, said "Yes, I remember your call. Could you wait here for a minute so that I can get the pamphlets." They nodded yes, and the man left them waiting at the front door. When the young man returned with the pamphlets, Mr. Horton was also at the door, standing behind the two younger men.

The young man with the pamphlets asked, "May I help you?" Mr. Horton responded, "Yes, I called earlier about doing some work, and I was told to come over around noon." The man said, "Yes, let me take care of these brothers first then I will be right with you." He told the two young men that the pamphlets would be four dollars. One of the young men handed him a ten-dollar bill. The man then excused himself again to retrieve change.

When he returned with the change, all three men were standing in the doorway. As the man extended his hand to give the two young men their change, all three pushed the man and made entrance inside the house. The two young men pulled their guns and they forced the man into the kitchen, the room adjacent to the front door. Mr. Horton stood at the front door waving his arm as a signal to the others in the cars to join them.

The five associates quickly walked to the house to join the three already inside of the premises. As the two young men followed the man into the kitchen with their guns positioned at his back, a young woman screamed. The young woman who screamed was already in the kitchen. She was feeding her eighteen-month-old daughter lunch in the kitchen when the men entered with her brother, brandishing pistols. One of the men yelled at her to shut up, then yanked her daughter from her arms, taking her out of the kitchen.

The other man told the woman, who was now sobbing heavily, to lie down on the floor. He ordered both her and her brother to lie down on the floor, and then he pulled the tablecloth from the table and placed it on top of their heads. The other men began to search the rest of the house, looking for people and valuables. The man who took the baby, went upstairs to the second floor where three of his associates sat with another man and woman and three young children.

Mr. Horton then asked the couple if there was anyone else in the house. They said no one else was there. He then asked where their leader was, and they said he went to run some errands. He said okay, and then we'll wait. The young man who brought the baby upstairs was told by

Mr. Horton to take the man and woman downstairs in the kitchen to lie on the floor with the first couple. The woman moved hesitantly and asked, "Why are you all doing this to us? What did we do to you? Mr. Horton smiled, and said, "Ask your leader; he knew we would come calling on him, ask him about that letter."

Then the young man marched the couple downstairs to the kitchen. The children, who had never seen any of these strange men in their house before, were crying. One child, a nine-day-old infant, was lying quietly on the bed wrapped in a blanket. He began to cry after hearing the cries from four other children in the room, his one-year old sister, his three-year-old brother, and his eighteen-month -old cousin.

While the children were crying and yelling for their "mommy" upstairs, shots could be heard that sounded like they came from just below where the kids were held. There were about eight shots in all, one fired right after the other. Frightened from the sound, the babies cried even louder.

Simultaneously, one of the men in the room with the children heard the scream, which sounded like an older child coming from another room on the second floor. He searched the other three rooms on that floor. As he entered the last room, he heard the whimpering of a child's voice emanating from the closet.

He opened the closet door and found an eleven-year-old little boy kneeling atop a stack of clothes. He heard all of the confusion occurring in the house and decided to seek shelter in the closet. He pleaded in a soft voice with the man not to hurt him. He said, "Please don't kill me sir."

Meanwhile the four little ones continued to cry loudly in the next room as they asked for their "mommy." Another gunshot was heard, and the children cried even louder than before. One of the associates in the room became annoyed by the children's loud screams for their mom, so he picked up the nine-day-old infant and took him into the bathroom. He returned three minutes later and picked up the one-year-old girl and the three-year-old boy, taking them into the bathroom. Loud screams were heard from the bathroom for about three minutes, then complete silence. The man returned to retrieve the last child left in the room, an eighteen-month-old little girl. He then took her into the bathroom; she cried like the others for the first three minutes. Then there was dead silence.

The eight men continued to walk around the house, emptying drawers looking for money and valuables. At approximately 3:45 p.m., the man thought to be "the leader" by the eight men in the house, returned home with his wife.

From his front door window, he was able to see intruders walking around his house. One of the intruders noticed the man at the door, so he attempted to unlock the door and pull the man and his wife inside, but he seemed to be having trouble with the lock. Noticing someone messing with the door as he and his wife attempted to enter, the man hollered out, "Who are you, and what are you doing in my house?" The intruder responded, "It's Tommy." The man hollered back, "I don't know any Tommy," and yelled at his wife to go next door and call the police.

After sending his wife to the neighbor's, the man then ran to his car parked in front of his house. As he reached his car, the eight intruders fearing the police's arrival began to run out of the house. Three men ran out of the back entrance running south from his backyard. Two men ran out of the front entrance going north, and three men ran out of the side entrance traveling south. Of the three who came out the side entrance, once was carrying a large blue suitcase, which he discarded because it slowed his running time.

The owner of the premise was now in his vehicle, and since his wife was phoning the police at the neighbor's, he decided to follow the two men that ran out of his front door in his direction. He thought they were burglars and figured he could hold them until the police arrived if he caught them,

He chased the two for a half a mile in his car as they ran on foot. Then one of the men turned toward his vehicle and fired a pistol in his direction. The sight of the pistol alarmed him, so he decided to let the police handle the capture. Suddenly a horrific feeling came over him. He thought about how frightened his children must be at home having seen these armed strangers.

He raced back home to check on his children and make sure everyone was safe. His wife sat at the neighbor's, nervously and impatiently waiting on the police's arrival. At 4:45 p.m., the neighbor's bell rang; it was two uniformed police officers. They asked the woman what the problem was, and she nervously described the shock she and her husband experienced upon their arrival from shopping.

She told the police how she and her husband witnessed intruders walking around their house, and how as she walked to the neighbor's house, she witnessed the same men running away, going in different directions. She then told the police how frightened she became after phoning her house to see if everyone was safe, and not getting an answer. The policemen asked her how many people are supposed to be at home, and she responded, "Nine." There should be five children, and four adults inside the house. The police asked that she remain at the neighbor's while they checked the house.

Before entering the house, the two policemen checked the surrounding area. They noticed the blue suitcase that was dropped by one of the intruders. One of the policemen opened the suitcase and found two sawed-off shotguns. There was also a brown-lunch bag filled with ammunition inside. His partner checked the back of the house where the woman said they saw three men running. There, the policemen recovered a small black handgun, a black top hat, and a brown bag with a newspaper. The policemen left the items in their place and returned to the squad car to call for backup in case some of the intruders were still on the premises.

There were so many clues left behind that one police officer remarked to the other, "Whoever burglarized this house would have done better to leave us a trail of crumbs to his house." The policemen had no idea that after entering the residence on 7700 16th street, they and the rest of Washington D.C. would never be the same again.

CHAPTER TWO

On the Killer's Trail

When the two officers went inside the house, there were no signs of intruders present, but the house seemed to have been ransacked. After checking the first floor for intruders they went down to the basement. They were sickened by what they saw.

Four bodies lying still with blood sprayed all over the room. The bodies were of two women and two men. They checked the pulses to find the two women both unconscious but still breathing. The men were dead.

One officer phoned in on his radio for an ambulance saying that there was a possible mass slaying at the address and that they would need an ambulance. The other officer went upstairs to check the second floor bedrooms. Two minutes later, the officer in the basement heard his partner, who was on the second floor scream, Oh, God!

He immediately ran upstairs with his weapon drawn. His partner had thrown up his lunch at the sign of the atrocities found in the bathroom. Three infant children were floating atop the water in the bathtub, and one very tiny child who looked to be a week old was floating on his stomach in the bathroom sink.

When they searched the bedrooms, they found nothing. Upon checking the bedroom closets, the officers found the last victim; a small boy who looked to be nine or ten kneeled down in the back of a closet as if he were hiding. He was also dead, with a gunshot to the head.

By this time, three homicide detectives had arrived on the scene along with five squad cars and two ambulances. Police had begun to cordon off the area with their crime scene tape as neighbors began coming outside to see what all the police activity was about. The detectives were baffled upon entry to the premises. The first response to a mass killing of a family members is to investigate the incident as a murder-suicide. Family members are always considered first suspects in most domestic tragedies. However, this was different. The detectives had no idea who these people were living in this very expensive house.

The two women were rushed to the nearest hospital, and at the same time the apparent owner was returning with his wife. He was very confused to see all the police activity at his house for what he thought to be a burglary. The detectives asked the man his name, and the name of the religious organization. The man replied, "I am Khaliffa Hamaas Abdul Khaalis, and this is our home." "Whose home?" replied the detective. "Our home, my family. We are Muslims. This is also the headquarters of our religion, which is Orthodox Islam. Where is my family?" asked Mr. Khaalis.

Two women were taken to the hospital, unconscious with gunshot wounds to the head. Two men and five children are still here in the house; they're all dead. Mrs. Khaalis screamed and fainted into the arms of her husband. Mr. Khaalis and the remaining two detectives began to lead the search of the area for clues and interview the neighbors. Two women who lived on either side of the Khaalis house were waiting to speak with detectives.

They had both witnessed two late model cars pull up about two doors from the house about 12:30 p.m. They saw four black men get out of each car. A total of eight well-dressed black men, most were tall, and dark sinned. They saw the first three men walk up to the door alone. Then the other five followed about five minutes later. They didn't hear any gunshots, and they saw no cause for alarm until they saw the men running out of the house about 4:00 p.m.

Two of the men apparently ran across the women's backyard dropping a large blue suitcase. Three of the eight men ran across another neighbor's yard, leaving a brown paper bag, two pistols and a top hat. This would turn out to be the biggest mass murder in the history of Washington, D.C.

The following morning, *The Washington Post* headlines read, "Seven Executed in Districts Biggest Mass Murder." Although the detectives were satisfied that this wasn't a murder-suicide and they apparently were left some clues with which to track the killers, they were still baffled about who the victims were and what the murders were all about.

Their first order of business was to check out the religious leader, and find out who owned the deed to the property. Since they had no criminal file on Mr. Khaalis, one of the Metropolitan detectives phoned a friend who happened to be in the F.B.I. He had this friend retrieve any information that the bureau was sure to have on anyone who professed to be a religious leader. The detective hit the jackpot.

His friend told him that Khaliffa Hamaas Abdul Khaalis was formerly Ernest McGhee, who was an associate of the late Malcolm X, and a former national secretary with the Nation of Islam. He also mentioned that Mr. Khaalis was a former jazz musician who toured with Charlie Parker and had converted to orthodox Islam about ten years earlier.

The detectives were trying to control the leaks about their investigation by keeping the leads within the confines of the metropolitan police department, but once they got the deed of ownership, they knew that they could no longer keep the investigation local.

A professional basketball player, who played for the Milwaukee Buck, named Lew Alcindor purchased the house in 1971, and later, changed his name to Kareem Abdul Jabbar. Thereafter Jabbar pledged his allegiance to the orthodox Islamic Faith and donated the $78,000 house to his spiritual leader of the Hanafi Madhhab, Imam Khaliffa Hamaas Abdul Khaalis.

The Hanafis were a small, relatively unknown group of black men and women, who contrary to the Nation of Islam, believed in the Orthodox form of Islam. They had no affiliation with the Nation of Islam, led by Elijah Muhammad, called "Black Muslims" by the press.

The Nation of Islam had a large membership, and a great deal of name recognition due in part to Malcolm X and Muhammad Ali. Kareem Abdul Jabbar's conversion to Orthodox Islam had given the Hanafis a little more recognition, but most people were still unaware of who they were. The detectives continued to question Mr. Khaalis, who was both teary-eyed and angry about the massacre of his family.

His wife, now conscious, lay on the couch and sobbed as the police questioned her husband. The homicide detective thought Mr. Khaalis' anger to be suspicious. Not suspicious in a way to make Mr. Khaalis a suspect, but to the detective, Mr. Khaalis acted as if he knew who the perpetrators were. Earlier, Mr. Khaalis shouted, "Those black, fake Muslims killed my babies." Having seen the perpetrators, the detective could understand Mr. Khaalis yelling out "black" since he witnessed the men leaving his house, but the "fake" didn't make any sense. He quietly wrote a note to himself as a reminder to mention the outburst to Mr. Khaalis when his mood was calmer.

The crime lab had recently finished photographing the house and bodies, and now the coroner waited for Khaalis to make the identification. Khaalis was taken to the basement to identify the adults first.

Khaalis, a physically strong man, with an aggressive demeanor, could barely contain his emotions as he identified the two men. (The women found unconscious had been taken in an ambulance to the hospital.) Khaalis looked down once and then pointed as tears shrieked down his face. He pointed, this is David Khaalis, "He's my son, he's twenty-five." He pointed again, "This is Abdul Nur, he's a good young man, he's a part of our community, he's twenty-three." Khaalis then told the detectives to get the bodies into the van; he didn't want his wife to see them.

Khaalis then led the detectives upstairs to the second floor, to view the bodies of the babies. The crime lab had finished their photography, but the bodies still were submerged in water. When Khaalis reached the top of the second floor, he paused then walked into the bathroom. Khaalis could no longer contain the tears. He screamed loudly, then put his head down and cried. Khaalis pulled himself together a few minutes later, and lambasted the detectives for leaving the bodies of the babies in the water. Khaalis put a towel on the bathroom floor and began to take the children out of the water. As he took each child out of the water, he identified it for the detectives. He took the nine-day-old infant from the sink, and said, "This is my little warrior, born last Tuesday on the 8th. This is little Abdul Tasibur Khaalis."

Then he took the children from the bathtub. He laid the little girls onto the towel. He said, "This is little Bibi, my princess, she's my granddaughter. This is Khadyja, my angel, she's eighteen months, and this warrior is my son Abdullah, he's two months short of three years old."

The police then took Mr. Khaalis to one of the bedrooms. There kneeled in a closet sat the last victim, Khaalis' other son, his pride and joy. Khaalis said, "This is my son Rahman

Uddein Khaalis, he's eleven." After that Khaalis broke down crying, he went into the adjacent room and shut the door while yelling, "Don't let my wife up here until you remove our children."

When the ambulance reached the hospital, the older woman, identified as Bibi Khaalis, Hamaas Khaalis' other wife,was still unconscious and bleeding. The second woman, who was shot in the head three times, was miraculously conscious and alert! A detective arrived at the hospital with hopes to speak with the young Ms. Khaalis before the doctors took her to surgery.

Detective Branson, a nine-year veteran who had worked on many murder cases in the city, walked into the operating room, where both Almina and Bibi were being prepared for surgery. Detective Branson identified himself to Almina Khaalis. The first thing Ms. Khaalis said to the Detective was, where's my daughter? Detective Branson wanted to wait for Almina's father Hamaas Khaalis to break the news about little Bibi, but Almina insisted that the Detective inform her of her daughter's whereabouts.

Detective Branson felt like he had no choice, but to give her the tragic news. He said, "I'm sorry to be the one to inform you of this, but your daughter, and your brothers and sisters are all dead." Almina screamed, and the doctors came running to her side. They told Detective Branson to leave, but he knew he couldn't leave until he asked Almina if she knew who the attackers were.

If Almina were to die during surgery without giving any information about the gunmen, the case could die with her. As the doctors began to wheel her over for surgery, Detective Branson moved to the foot of the gurney. He said, "Guys, this is the only conscious witness who may be able to identify the killers of seven people. I need two minutes please!" The senior surgeon said, "Take your two minutes, detective."

Detective Branson walked over towards Almina's head and put his hand on her shoulder. He told her, "I know you're in a lot of pain right now Almina, both physically and emotionally. I need your help now, if we're going to catch these killers I need to know anything you can tell me."

Almina, still sobbing, said they were "Elijah Poole's cutthroat gang." Detective Branson responded, "Who?" Almina repeated, "Elijah Poole's cutthroat gang." Then she said in an agitated tone, "They were Black Muslims, detective! Is that better for you?" "How do you know that they were Black Muslims?" the detective asked. "I know they were Black Muslims because one of the men asked about a letter that my father wrote to the Black Muslim ministers." "What did he ask about the letter?" asked the Detective. "He asked me why did my father write those letters, and why didn't I stop him." "Do you know how many men there were in total?" he asked. Almina said she only saw the first three who entered the house, but she said she heard voices upstairs to indicate that there were more than five.

Detective Branson's last question to Almina before the doctors wheeled her away was to ask her if she could identify the three perpetrators that she saw. Her responses were, not all three, but definitely two. She said she would never forget that man who yanked her baby from her arms. She identified him as a dark skinned black male of about medium height and a thin build. She said he had a thin mustache, and was wearing a black coat with black leather gloves. The other man she said appeared to be the leader, he gave the others instructions. He was taller, about six feet and light skinned. She added that he had no facial hair and was wearing a brown wool coat with green slacks and green crocodile loafers.

Detective Branson took Almina's hand and squeezed it lightly, and then he thanked her, wishing a speedy recovery. The detectives, though visibly shocked after witnessing the aftermath of such a horrific crime, were savoring their victory of gathering so much evidence within a matter of hours. They were hot on the case.

Detective Branson and his partner Detective Jacobs were inspecting the box of evidence left at the scene. A 38 caliber known in the street as a "Saturday night special" was sent to ballistics. The two sawed-off rifles were sent to the fingerprint lab, and then to ballistics. The top hat and suitcase was also sent to the fingerprint lab. Detective Branson and Jacobs thought it would only be a matter of hours before they found their killers. They had the murder weapons in their custody. They knew what time the murders occurred, and they were also beginning to understand why the murders were committed.

They surmised what the Khaalis' already knew, that the murders were committed as a punishment for Hamaas Khaalis sending letters to leaders of the Nation of Islam. As both Detectives Branson and Jacobs sat at their desk reviewing the evidence, they both had the same thought, and shouted it in unison, "We must get a copy of the letter." Detective Branson smiled at his partner thinking about their telepathic experience. Then he said, "Let's wait until tomorrow. Let the Khaalis family catch their breath, then we'll get a copy of the letter from Hamaas Khaalis.

CHAPTER THREE

The Letter

On Sunday, January 21st, only three days after the horrific murders, Detective Branson and Jacobs decided to retrieve Mr. Khaalis' letter. When they arrived, Mr. Khaalis was in his kitchen eating breakfast. He welcomed the two detectives inside and said, "I guess you're here for my letter."

Detective Branson noticed that Mr. Khaalis' mood was much calmer and more pleasant. Detective Jacobs responded to Mr. Khaalis' statement, he said, "How did you know we were here for the letter?" Mr. Khaalis said, "That's the only explanation I could come up with for why you would darken my doorstep on Sunday morning. You need to know the motive, am I right?" Detective Branson told Mr. Khaalis that his guess was correct. Then he took out his notebook looking for the notes he wrote about the initial investigation. Detective Branson remembered that he needed to ask Mr. Khaalis about a statement he made in regard to the killers.

As Mr. Khaalis attempted to get up from breakfast to retrieve a copy of the letter, Detective Branson said, "Before you get us the letter, I must ask you a question about a statement you made on Thursday." Mr. Khaalis looked at the detective with a puzzling stare, and said, "I'm listening." Detective Branson continued, he said, "On Thursday, you shouted, "Them fake Black Muslims killed my babies." Forgive me if I am incorrect, but it sounded to me as if you had some familiarity with the perpetrators." Mr. Khaalis looked at the detective angrily and said, "Is that what you learned from detective school?" He continued, "I don't know the killers personally, detective, we're not pen pals, but obviously I have an idea of who sent them."

Detective Jacobs responded with an arrogant tone, "Well, who do you think sent them?" Mr. Khaalis responded, "You interviewed my daughter in the hospital, did you not? I'm sure she told you what the killers said when she asked why they were in our home."

Losing patience with the detectives, Mr. Khaalis told them to wait while he retrieved the letter. When he returned, he said, "Now you have my daughter's statement, and you have a copy of my letter, all that's left to do is for you to find these guys and leave us alone. Now please leave our home."

Detective Branson apologized for any inconsideration, and he along with his partner headed for the door. As they were leaving Mr. Khaalis said, "One minute detectives. I guess I should tell you that I am holding a news conference tomorrow to expose the killers to the press. Detective Jacobs turned around to face Mr. Khaalis, as he tried to keep his composure, he said "Mr. Khaalis, if you go to the press naming people that you believe to be behind the killings, you can be sued for slander and defamation of character without any substantial proof of their guilt."

Mr. Khaalis just stared at them coldly and said, "Well, I guess you guys better get to work on those clues. You've got twenty-four hours before I go to the press. Detectives Branson and Jacobs headed back to the department to begin reading the letter.

In the car Detective Jacobs replied, "That Khaalis is really a piece of work, isn't he?" Detective Branson continued to drive, never responding to his partner's comment. Back at the police department, the detectives sat down with coffee and began to read Mr. Khaalis' three-page letter sent to ministers of the Nation of Islam.

In the introduction of the letter, Mr. Khaalis described Elijah Muhammad, the spiritual leader of the Nation of Islam, as a lying deceiver. The rest of the letter gets progressively more insulting.

In the body of the letter, Mr. Khaalis goes into a litany of reasons as to why the Nation of Islam's basic tenets are false. He began with the main members of the Nation believed to be Allah in disguise. The doctrine of The Nation of Islam exposes that W.D. Fard gave Elijah Poole the teachings of Islam. Elijah Poole then converted to Islam from Christianity. Then he changed his name to Elijah Muhammad. Fard and Muhammad opened a Muslim temple in Detroit in 1933, then Fard mysteriously disappeared. Elijah Muhammad opened the second temple in Chicago, thus spreading the faith of Islam.

Khaalis described Elijah Muhammad's enlightenment as mythological nonsense. He also ridiculed the leader W.D. Fard, calling him a "slightly cockeyed criminal," while referring to Elijah Muhammad as "laden with sin." Addressing a question directly to the ministers, Khaalis asked, "What madness is in your leader and teacher Muhammad, what kind of minds do you have, to be deaf, dumb, and blind to everything." Khaalis continued his litany of insults, now directed at the entire membership. He wrote, "Followers of Muhammad are eaters of their brother's flesh, and Black Muslims have polluted minds and will burn forever in violently hot flame."

In the final summation of his critique of the Nation of Islam, Khaalis redirects his final insult back to the leadership of Elijah Muhammad. He stated that, 'Elijah Muhammad had no more authority to claim to be a prophet of Allah than did Elijah Pitts," a former Green Bay Packer football player.

Detectives Branson and Jacobs finished reading the letter almost simultaneously. They looked up at each other and nodded, then Detective Branson said, "We've got a motive." Neither detective had knowledge of Islamic doctrine, outside of what they read in the papers about the

"Black Muslims." After agreeing with his partner, Detective Jacobs commented, "That Khaalis sure has some balls on him, but I bet a year's salary that today he wished that he wasn't such a persuasive writer."

On Monday, January 22nd, the ballistic report was in. The report confirmed that the weapons found outside the house were indeed the murder weapons. A partial print on one of the weapons was confirmed as well. A print found on the sawed-off shotgun, which showed no match to known felons in Washington, was sent out to three nearby cities, Baltimore, New York, and Philadelphia. They matched a known felon from Philadelphia. The newspaper found at the scene was also a Philadelphia newspaper, which was not sold in Washington in 1973. The evidence was coming in at a perfect pace for Detective Branson. Now he could tell the press that they were following a lead that the killers were out-of-towners.

At six o'clock Mr. Khaalis, who was dressed in all black, gave a press conference from his living room. The print, television, and radio mediums were all present to hear Mr. Khaalis' first public remarks about the loss of his family. Mr. Khaalis' voice was very strong. He briefly introduced himself, and the organization, and then Mr. Khaalis got to the order of business.

Sounding similar to the late Malcolm X, who eight years earlier accused the members of The Nation of Islam of firebombing his house, upon the orders of Elijah Muhammad, Mr. Khaalis got right to the point. (Malcolm X would be assassinated a week after his accusations.)

He told the press about the letters he sent to seventy-seven Black Muslim temples, addressed to the ministers. Then he stated that he believed the killings were in retaliation to the letter. Then, Mr. Khaalis asked the reporters if they had any questions. One of the reporters asked Mr. Khaalis directly, if he thought the order to murder his family was given by Elijah Muhammad. Mr. Khaalis said, absolutely. The reporters were finished with Mr. Khaalis, so Detective Branson stood up to tell them about the progress of the investigation. Detective Branson cleared his throat, greeted the press, and began his monologue.

He told the press that they had reason to believe that the men responsible for the murders of seven people were from outside of Washington, D.C. He hadn't prepared to disclose the location of the suspects, but three reporters known for leaking police information were present, so he decided to beat them to the punch. He paused for a second, and said, "We believe the perpetrators are from Philadelphia, based on the evidence from ballistics, and eye witness testimony of neighbors who observed suspects' license plates." A television reporter asked, "Is the metropolitan police department working with detectives in Philadelphia to find the killers?" Detective Branson responded, "Yes, we are. In fact, we've recently sent two detectives to Philadelphia to bring us back some photographs." The press conference closed with Detective Branson assuring Mr. Khaalis that his department would do everything possible to track down his family's killers.

When Detective Branson returned to the station, two FBI agents were waiting for him in his office. Detective Branson glanced at the agents disapprovingly, being transparent about the fact that he did not appreciate them being let into his office when he was not there.

Detective Branson told them about all the evidence they had leading to Philadelphia. One of the agents got up and closed Detective Branson's door, not wanting anyone to hear what he was about to say. In a whisper, he told Detective Branson that the FBI was going to give them an agent to utilize for the investigation.

The agent, fearing a federal coup d'état, said, "This guy would be uniquely beneficial to your investigation." "Why is that?" asked Detective Branson. "We have agents in place, who have successfully infiltrated The Nation of Islam temples through undercover work," the agent responded. Detective Branson said, "Oh, a secret spy. Well, I'll tell you what, we will use your guy, but we're going to send one of our own up to Philadelphia's temple as well."

Detective Branson thanked the agents and showed them to the door. He suspected that they had another agenda in offering their services, so he requested a young, black detective to report to his office.

Remus Williams, a five-year police veteran, had only joined the homicide unit as a detective a year ago. At twenty-six years old, he was the youngest in the unit. He was also black, which meant that he suddenly would become the most important person in the Hanafi murder investigation.

CHAPTER FOUR

Top of the Clock

Remus Williams reported to work at eight o'clock on Wednesday, January 24th. He hadn't even taken his jacket off, nor had his customary morning coffee when he was summoned to a meeting with Detective Branson.

Remus and a twenty-year veteran named Vincent Combs were the only black detectives assigned to the homicide unit. Vincent, being the elder officer, was tolerant to the many racial epithets both he and the young Remus were subject to from their fellow officers. Remus, who was often called "Uncle Remus," after the fictional slave character, had considered leaving the force on occasion because of the disrespect of the white officers. As Remus walked to Branson's office, he wondered why he was summoned. He knew Branson and his ten-man team were working on the Hanafi case, and he didn't think they wanted a rookie homicide detective joining their investigation.

Detective Branson was all smiles when detective Williams walked into his office. He wasted little time. He said, "Remus, we need you desperately in the Hanafi case." Detective Williams was a little circumspect. He said, "You need me? Why?" Branson told him about the FBI's visit, and the subsequent proposal. Detective Williams stated the case before Branson could finish the next sentence. He said, "Oh, so you need good Ole Uncle Remus to be a spook, huh?" Detective Branson looked at Remus grinning, and said, "If that's what you want to call it, sure, we need you to infiltrate Philadelphia's Temple #12."

Detective Branson and his ten-man team were sure the killers were from Philadelphia, based on the evidence. So it stood to reason that if they were from Philadelphia, and they were Black Muslims, then they had to be members of Temple #12.

Detective Williams was on the train to Philadelphia that evening. He arrived in Philadelphia with a crew cut, a blue suit, and a gray bow tie. Detective Williams became nervous as he got himself ready to attend his first meeting at Temple #12.

Before becoming a police officer, Detective Williams traveled to Philadelphia to visit his cousins. They would stand out on the corner singing "Doo Wap" harmonies, as they competed with other local groups. He hadn't been to Philadelphia since he became a cop in 1968, but he knew a few of his cousins had become Muslims. He knew how they felt about the police, and the entire white establishment, so he didn't bother to tell any of his cousins in Philly that he had joined the force. He didn't bother to tell Detective Branson that he had cousins who may be members of Temple #12 either. He wanted the assignment, and he knew that they could exclude him on the basis of conflict of interest, if they knew otherwise.

Detective Williams had heard many rumors about the reputations of some of the Muslims affiliated with Temple #12. There were two prevalent nicknames people used when describing some of the brothers from Temple #12. One was very flattering, and the other was ominous. The former nickname given to Temple #12 was "Top of the Clock."

Accounts have it that Elijah Muhammad himself coined Temple #12 "Top of the Clock," upon visiting the Temple for one of his annual speeches. Supposedly, Elijah Muhammad visited the Temple and observing the sharp, disciplined style of the Fruit of Islam, (male members of the Nation of Islam) called them the "Top of the Clock" in comparison to the other temples he observed.

The phrase stuck, and took on a life of its own. From that point on, visiting ministers would receive a roar from the audience when they shouted the words, "Top of the Clock!" One member recalls a minister visiting Temple #12, and receiving a standing ovation after he shouted, "Temple #12, you are head and shoulders above the rest. You are the pace setters, other Temples on the east coast look to you to set the standard because you are the Top of the Clock!" The other nickname Detective Williams had heard, as a description of Temple #12 members were that of "Death Squad."

Temple #12 was also known as the Death Squad because some of the high-ranking members of the Temple were known to be associated with an emerging group in Philadelphia known as the Black Mafia. In the late 1960's, a group of young black men from South and North Philadelphia, who were ex-convicts, had converted to Islam while in prison. They were some of the so-called rehabilitated members, to which the ministers were claiming credit for turning their lives around.

Upon release from prison, a handful of the newly converted Muslims, who were devoted to a life of criminal activity, decided to extort legitimate black businesses for protection money. They also decided that if heroin was going to be sold in the black community, they would control the distribution. Heroin was the main drug of choice in the poor black neighborhoods of Philadelphia in the late 1960's and early 1970's. They were not only extorting businesses and selling heroin, but also robbing banks and handling contract killings. The contract killings attributed to the Black Mafia Muslims were the catalyst for the term, "Death Squad."

Detective Williams arrived at his cousins that evening, on January 24th. His cousin Paul, who hadn't seen him in five years, answered the door and greeted his cousin, who stood in front of him in a dark blue suit and gray bow tie. Paul said, "Well, I'll be damn, As-Salaam-Alaikum brother." Detective Williams smiled and replied, "Wa-Alaikum-As-Salaam." They went inside, and chatted for two hours, catching up on the last five years.

After discussing family, Paul asked, "So what brings you to Philly from D.C. cous?" Remus replied, "Man, I just got into Islam about ten months ago, and I've been really enjoying my rebirth. But since those kids were killed in D.C., a lot of us have been harassed and threatened, so I just decided to check Temple #12 out for a while until things cool off in D.C." Then Remus asked his cousin if he could stay with him for a few weeks. Paul was ecstatic, he said, "Of course you can stay, brother. Once you hear the teachings at the Top of the Clock, you may pull up from D.C. all together."

Remus wondered what Paul knew, and was hoping that his cousin was not involved. Remus asked Paul if they were also being harassed by the police. Paul responded, "No man, but some of the brothers are a little shaky because of yesterday's article that said the killers were from here." Trying not to sound too inquisitive, Remus asked, "What do you think?" Paul said, "What I think, and what I know are of no significance."

The next night, Paul took Remus to the Temple to hear the minister and meet some of the brothers. The Fruit of Islam security team looked very impressive to Remus. Most of them were tall, handsome, young black men, wearing very expensive suits. There were four of them on the podium with the minister, two stood directly behind the minister, and the other two stood on either side. The minister of Temple #12 was very popular. The minister's name was Jeremiah Shabazz.

Jeremiah Shabazz had just returned to his native Philadelphia in 1972. He returned to Temple #12 after being away for some years. He was credited, along with the late Malcolm X, for establishing Temple #12 in 1954. In 1959, Elijah Muhammad sent the young minister to Atlanta to spread the word of Islam throughout the South. Minister Shabazz was very successful in recruiting many black southerners into the Nation of Islam. Minister Shabazz became the top official for the southern temples, and also became a part of Elijah Muhammad's inner circle.

Remus recognized one of the guards behind Minister Shabazz, as an acquaintance of his cousins. He asked Paul, "Who is the short dark skin guy standing behind the minister? I recognize him from your neighborhood." Paul said, "Oh, that's Bubbles." Remus tried to remember why he was called "Bubbles." He said, "Paul, what's his real name?" Paul said, "James Price, you remember him, he used to fight all the time, then after you stopped coming to Philly, he got jammed up on a murder case, but he beat it. Ever since then, Bubbles has been going around trying to be this killer."

Remus's heart was beating like a lovesick teenager. He felt like he hit pay dirt. Somehow he knew James Price was involved in the Hanafi murders. If he wasn't involved, he would definitely know who was. At that point, Remus decided to get reacquainted with James "Bubbles" Price. The next few weeks with his new best friend would prove very fruitful to the investigation. James Price was a five and a half-foot, father of four, who wore a gun holster as a display of his Napoleonic complex.

After the minister's speech, Remus went up to shake his hand, as a way of get close to James Price. He told Minister Shabazz how much he appreciated the message. The minister thanked him and began to walk off the podium. The F.O.I. guards walked behind the minister.

As James Price came off the podium, Remus, still standing, said, "As-Salaam-Alaikum, brother Bubbles." James looked in his direction, uncertain of where he knew Remus from, and he responded, "Wa-Alaikum-As-Salaam." James then said, "Where do I know you from, brother?" Remus looking for strange responses shouted, "You don't remember me from Washington, brother?" James Price looked back with a menacing stare then he looked around at his fellow F.O.I. brothers from the podium, who were also looking strangely at Remus.

Getting the response he hoped for, Remus corrected his statement. He said, "I'm Paul's cousin from Washington, remember we used to sing together as teenagers?" James Price smiled a sigh of relief and said, "Oh yeah, brother Remus, brother Remus, you have to be careful how you say things in here, brother." Remus knew he had struck gold.

After the meeting, he invited James Price to the local diner, to catch up on old times. James Price was still the boastful wannabe, tough guy he tried so hard to be as a teenager. James was an illiterate, high school dropout, with an I.Q. of about 75. Remus knew that it wouldn't be hard to get James to tell him what he knew. He remembered that James liked to drink, so he took him down to a local bar one night, with the hopes of getting James to let his guard down. He told James to drive to a bar in South Philly, because a brother was supposed to meet him there to bring him two hundred dollars. He told James that he'd split the money with him.

They arrived about nine o'clock. Remus, trying to buy some time, said, "Man, we must be early, you want to get a little drink while we wait?" James replied, "I know that I shouldn't, but a little drink won't hurt anybody." Then Remus went into a soliloquy about how the police in Washington were harassing all the Black Muslims, and that whoever killed the Khaalis family saved the brothers in Washington's temple the trouble, because they were planning to kill them as well.

James Price smiled, and said, "You're welcome." "Do you mean you did that thing?" asked Remus. James Price, still smiling, said, "Yeah man, what do you think!" Remus feigning his disgust said, 'Wow, brother, thank you but I know you didn't do that thing alone. Who else do I owe a deal of gratitude to?" James Price replied, "Oh, many others, you met some of them last night." Remus decided to play ignorant, he said, "You're kidding me, man. I didn't meet any of the guys involved in that thing." James Price being led like a mouse to the pied piper, without any realization, gave Remus the names of his partners in crime. He rattled off seven names of his fellow Muslim brothers and said, they were all in Washington with me on the caper.

Remus had recorded the conversation at the bar, with a micro-tape recorder he had strapped to his leg. He had received enough information from James Price to return to the capital. That evening, Remus phoned in his findings to Detective Branson, then he went to Philadelphia's 30th Street Station to board the train back to Washington.

Branson and his ten-man team were at the train station waiting for Remus to give him a hero's welcome. The investigation had reached a crucial stage. The detectives would have to proceed slowly in order to make their case stick against the eight suspects.

It would take several weeks before the detectives would be able to get subpoenas to bring the suspects in for a line-up. Meanwhile, Philadelphia's Death Squad would wreak havoc in the city of brotherly love and in New Jersey on a go for broke crime spree.

CHAPTER FIVE
Going for Broke

One might guess that a group of known felons, who were also known as Black Muslims to law enforcement, would hide under a rock after all the publicity in the search for the Hanafi murderers. Not so for the Philadelphia death squad. The massacre in Washington must have given them the attitude of invulnerability, because after the massacre, the suspects went on a crime binge that would make Bonnie and Clyde envious.

On February 8, 1973, only three weeks after the Hanafi murders, a Philadelphia family became the next target. Ernest Kelly, a former number's writer who successfully transitioned himself into a saloon owner, made the dreadful mistake one night of boasting about how much money he had stashed away since going into the saloon business. Ernest Kelly, who was originally from North Philadelphia, was well loved in his West Oak Lane Tavern. On many occasions the patrons would come to Kelly's bar just to hear the greatly embellished rags to riches story Ernest Kelly was sure to tell. Ernest enjoyed talking about himself, and his customers enjoyed listening.

Ernest had a son who came into the tavern and helped his father run the business. Ernest's son was Barry Kelly. A few years earlier, Barry had become a member of the Nation of Islam. He changed his name to Abdul Muhammad, but his father would only call him Barry. Although Barry didn't drink, his affiliation with the Nation of Islam would attract other young Black Muslims to the tavern, who didn't drink either. They would sit at the bar, sometimes listening to Ernest stories, other times trying to recruit new members of the Nation. This angered Ernest because he saw this as a hindrance to his business. Not that the Muslims would convince patrons to stop drinking and join the temple, but that they would convince patrons to take their business elsewhere for fear of receiving a sermon at Kelly's when they received their drinks.

One evening in late January 1973, after retelling his story of an impoverished childhood, Ernest did something that he would later come to regret. He gave a dollar amount of his worth. After telling a few customers how he walked four miles everyday after school to a nearby market where he'd bag groceries for nickels, a patron said to him, "Enough of the Horatio Alger story, Ernest. I want to know how much money you've made out of this place?" Ernest smiled, and then said, "Well, I've got $100,000 stashed in a safe deposit box, so I must be doing alright."

About four members from Temple #12 were sitting at the bar that evening when Ernest made his confession.

A couple of days later, two Muslims visited Ernest. They informed Ernest that they were collecting protection money from business owners whose particular type of business was considered to be undesirable by the Muslims. They told him that the bar owners in the area were paying five hundred dollars a week to stay in business, and that failure to pay would result in something terrible happening to the tavern, or worst to Ernest. Ernest stared at the two men, who were his son's age. He told the men that he had nothing for them, and that he would not be intimidated. Ernest was an old hustler from the 1940's; he didn't take kindly to being extorted by those he considered to be children. He told the men to leave his establishment and never come back.

A few days later, Ernest had forgotten the incident and was back to his old boastful self. On the morning of February 8, 1973, Ernest was at his home in the West Oak lane section of Philadelphia. He received a knock on the door. When he opened the door, he saw four impeccably well-dressed young black men on his porch, with guns drawn and demanding entry. When they entered the house, they told Ernest that they had just "upped the ante," and five hundred dollars a week was not going to be enough. They wanted the $100,000 cash stashed in a safe deposit box.

The leader of the four, identified as John Clark, told Ernest that the other three men would stay at his home with his wife, children, and grandchildren while he escorted Ernest to the bank to withdraw the money. John Clark warned him that if he did anything stupid at the bank, he would return home to a blood bath.

As Ernest rode to the bank with John Clark, who had a reputation in the street as a cold killer, Ernest thought to himself that even if he turned the money over to these guys, there was still a great possibility that his family wouldn't get out alive. So when Ernest entered the bank, he slipped a note to the guard as he approached the safe deposit box. He managed to write the note as he filled out a slip to open his box. The note read that he was being forced to come to the bank and empty his safe deposit box by the man standing at the bank's entry. The quick thinking guard alerted the police of a bank robbery. The police arrived within minutes.

As Ernest Kelly left the bank with $100,000 in a bag, and John Clark standing behind him with a gun at his back, the police pulled to the scene with sirens. John Clark pushed Ernest Kelly out of his path and fired shots at the police, as he ran away from the scene. Ernest Kelly immediately ran to the police and informed them of what was occurring at his residence. The police called in for a few unmarked vehicles to be sent to Ernest's house. They didn't want to send patrol cars for fear that the kidnappers might start killing the Kellys out of desperation.

Two patrol cars at the scene went in pursuit of John Clark, who was running on foot. Clark ran down a narrow driveway and the police lost chase. Ernest Kelly returned to his home in an unmarked police vehicle, escorted by three detectives. He entered his house through the basement door. The three detectives followed Ernest into the house through the basement. When they reached the first floor, they surprised the two gunmen who were sitting on the couch watching television. One gunman was captured as he used the bathroom. Ernest Kelly's wife, children, and grandchildren were all safe and unharmed.

The three men captured at the Kelly residence were identified as William Christian, Richard Dabney, and John Griffin. John Clark was captured a few days later after Ernest Kelly identified his photo. They were all arraigned and held on $100,000 dollars bail each. Since half of them were in custody at this time, the investigators would have an easier time identifying who was in Washington during the carnage, but their detainment would be short lived.

The following month the Philadelphia Yellow Cab Company, the city's largest service, was robbed in a holdup. The two robbers got away with fifty-two thousand dollars in cash. The next day a young thin black man arrived in the office of a bail bondsman. The young black man, who identified himself as Jerome Sinclair, gave the bail bondsman forty thousand dollars, which was the ten percent required to release each of the four kidnapping suspects. A few days after the four suspects were released, Jerome Sinclair's picture was identified as being one of the two gunmen who robbed the Yellow Cab Company.

James Price, another temple #12 member and a suspect in the Hanafi Killings, decided to build a war chest of "get away" cash of his own. On April 5, 1973, three men walked into the Baldwin Frankford Diaries office, located in the northeast section of Philadelphia. The three men commanded the six employees to lie down on the floor and empty their pockets. They took cash and credit cards out of the employees' wallets as well as five thousand dollars out of the office safe. They also relieved the employees of their jewelry, as they left the building.

The next day, the same three men, identified by Baldwin Dairies employees, were seen running from the Abrams Metal Company, in the Southwest section of the city. The owner, Myer Abrams was shot to death as he walked into his office, totally unaware that his company was being robbed. One of the three men identified in both robberies was James Henry Price. Price, who was only twenty-three years old, had racked up quite a lengthy yellow sheet since his days as a teenager.

In January 1969, James Price, then nineteen, and three of his friends were charged with the murder of an immigrant gas station owner. Charles Ben Ami, a forty-five year old Czechoslovakian Jew, had arrived in 1962 to seek his fortune. Ami's parents were slaughtered in the Nazis' death camps when he was a teenager. He was released when the allied forces liberated the camps in 1945. He came to America seventeen years later, after failed attempts to make a life in post-war Europe. He arrived in Philadelphia with his wife, and their ten-year-old son, Michael. Upon arrival, he purchased a garage in West Oak Lane, where he, an expert auto mechanic, would work for seven years building the shop into a thriving business.

On January 23, 1969 at 9:30 PM Charles Ben Ami began to lock up for the night. As he was locking up, four black men walked up to him, one pulled out a gun and demanded the cash receipts. Ami refused and the gunman shot him three times, once in the chest, once in the stomach, and once in the back. The police located three of the suspects almost immediately. All three suspects confessed, and named their fourth co-conspirator, James Price as the shooter.

The case was highly publicized, and the Philadelphia Jewish Community was enraged that Mr. Ami who lost his family, and almost lost his own life at the hands of the Nazis, would come to Philadelphia only to be gunned-down like an animal. James Price was brought in and interrogated. Price said nothing to the investigating detectives, and was released in his father's custody after his father posted bail.

As Price was leaving, a detective stated that he overheard Price confess to his father that he had indeed shot Charles Ben Ami. The police attempted to use his confession to his father as evidence. The judge threw out the confession, asserting that it violated his constitutional right under the new "Miranda ruling." Charges against Price were dropped, but his three co-defendants were convicted.

A few Philadelphia lawmen would later remark that they never knew until 1973 how much they would regret losing the case against James Price in 1969, and setting him loose on the public to be charged with murdering eight more people. James Price, John Clark, and the others were wreaking havoc on the city of Philadelphia with their crime binge, but it hadn't gotten the notice of the Washington investigators enough to make a link to the Hanafi murders.

This changed in June 1973. Ronald Harvey, suspected as being the leader of the pack from Temple #12, would commit another multiple homicide that was sure to get the attention from both local and Federal Law enforcement agencies--the murder of Major Coxson.

CHAPTER SIX
The Maje

There's been a lot written about Major Coxson in the almost 50 years since his death. He's been called a gangster, an entrepreneur and a confidence man. What's less known about the illusive "Maj" as he was affectionately called by friends and strangers were his very humble beginnings. Major Benjamin Coxsom (I'm not sure in the family lineage when the name Coxsom became Coxson), was born on June 20, 1928, to Israel and Maybell Coxsom. His father Israel, was born in the Gullah region of South Carolina around 1888. His mother Maybell was born around 1890 and hailed from Georgia. From all accounts, the married Coxsoms migrated to a small Pennsylvania mining town called Filbert, in Redstone Township. The Coxsom's first child Israel, named after his father, was two years older than Major, the middle child with a younger brother named Hosea. The three Coxson boys were educated in the integrated mining community. All the Coxson boys were thought of as good students for the era, but Major was thought to be an exceptional student, most notably with his ability to communicate. Major attended Redstone High school near his home town of Filbert, up until his junior year. In fact, he was elected president of his junior class, in this town with less than a ten percent population of Negroes. Prior to starting his senior year of high school, the Coxson's moved to Philadelphia. So in his senior year of high school, Major attended Benjamin Franklin high school, an all boy school in North Philadelphia. For many reasons noted in this chapter and beyond, I believe this is where many got a sense of Major's personality, as well as his motivations.

At the start of his senior year, Major got a job as a carhop at a center city restaurant. Due to his twelve hour work schedule, Major was given permission to attend school for only two hours a day. Even with the truncated schedule, Major was able to make himself known as a school leader. He ran for the position of class president in the fall of 1945. Even though he was attending high school in the big city, Benjamin Franklin was less integrated racially in 1945 than Major's previous school Redstone. There were a large number of German and Polish students attending Ben Franklin from the Port Richmond and Kensington sections of Philadelphia. There were also a great number of Italians attending Ben Franklin from South Philadelphia. In fact, there were two classmates of Major Coxson at Ben Franklin high school who would figure permanently throughout his life, and subsequent death investigation.

Jeremiah Pugh, known in high school as Jerry, was a high school classmate of Major Coxson. Jeremiah had come to Ben Franklin from the Negro section of North Philadelphia as a freshman student. Another student to arrive at Ben Franklin high as a freshman was a petite Italian boy named Nicodemo Scarfo (Nicky Scarfo), who at the time performed in amateur boxing exhibitions.

To his own admission, Major had stolen so much from his twelve hour a day carhop job while in school, that come the spring of 1946 he was able to purchase his first Cadillac for $800.00. According to classmates, Jeremiah wasn't initially happy about Major's arrival at Ben Franklin. Major seemed to have a privileged presence with his Cadillac and shortened schedule, in a space with very few Negroes and at times when they were supposed to be marginal at best.

When Major began his run for the title of class president, he was said to have reached out to all the Negro students first, hoping to receive favor in his candidacy based on race. However, Jeremiah was a notable standout in Major's political rally. Major would recall the incident later in his life to friends that he didn't realize until his senior year of high school that Negroes could be each other's worst enemy. He thought Jeremiah was jealous of his ascension at Franklin, and was attempting to derail his candidacy for class president by working with one of the white candidates. Much like Malcolm X's story of becoming class president, as he was thoroughly integrated into the rural white community, where he was educated formally to the 8th grade. So too were Major Coxson's experiences, having to lean on white support at Redstone high school in order to win the junior class president title. Major had no problem reaching across the racial aisle for support. In Ben Franklin, Major found himself needing to find support due in part to his miscalculation of support from Jeremiah Pugh. He found support and solidarity with the little scrawny Nicky Scarfo, who matched Major in height as well as in their equal desire for power and the finer things in life. Nicky Scarfo wasn't considered to be a highly intelligent student at Ben Franklin, but he seemed to enjoy the brotherhood being offered in general through the high school, and in specific through Major.

So Major Coxson leaned on his new friend to help him garner support for his class president candidacy amongst the other Italians at Ben Franklin, who didn't necessarily care for their fellow German or Jewish classmates running against Major. Matching the numerical outcomes of the big city political machines of the day, Major won with more votes than the number of students enrolled at Ben Franklin high school in 1946. No one knows what Major Coxson promised Nicky Scarfo to garner his support in 1946, nor if the promise had been fulfilled. However, what is known is the friendship between Major Coxson and Nicky Scarfo would endure for at least twenty five years, and served as the unknown linchpin for Major's ability to do business with various members of La Cosa Nostra, including Nicky Scarfo's soon to be boss Angelo Bruno. Incidentally, Nicky Scarfo graduated from Ben Franklin high school a year after Major Coxson in 1947, and according to law enforcement, was inducted for full membership into La Cosa Nostra by Joseph Ida then acting boss of the Philadelphia crime family just seven years later.

After high school, Major went on to attend Florida A&M University, on a full scholarship. Perhaps, his desire to set the academic world on its side served as the motivation for Major's run as class president, as a way to boost his college application. Unfortunately for Major, the initial motivation wasn't enough to allow him to remain in college. He left Florida A&M after only six weeks of matriculation. After his departure from college, Major returned to Philadelphia and took another job as a carhop. This time at a 7th & Chestnut by the Gimbels department store chain. Major had acquired a great adoration for automobiles, and was now parking cars for the Gimbel's lot. In a little time, he was given permission to wash cars on the lot. With the cost of a few buckets and sponges, Major expanded his car washing business to eight additional parking lots in downtown Philadelphia. In a short time, he had one hundred men working for him in his car washing business.

Abu described when he first heard about Major, who by this time had become a legend for his business acumen. After his successful car washing enterprise, Major rented a lot and began leasing cars. During the late 1940's and early 1950's it was very difficult for Black people to obtain loans for housing or automobiles, thus many Black Philadelphians were renting houses and apartments, but were hard pressed to find car dealerships to grant loans for car purchases. Understanding the need, Coxson began leasing vehicles from other car dealerships himself, but not just any vehicle, luxury vehicles. Coxson was leasing what he knew the Black hustlers in the city wanted to drive, Cadillacs and Lincoln Continentals. Abu called Major's hustle, "the wait game." The wait game involved Coxson leasing the vehicles in his name, and subleasing the vehicle to a hustler who could afford "the big bang up front" (a large down payment). Major would charge hustlers $2,000 or $3,000 down in the 1950's and 1960's for a vehicle that may have only cost him $400 to lease for the whole year. Understanding the mentalities and behaviors of many in the game, Major had no expectations that they would maintain the loan past six months, which would allow him to sublease the same vehicle maybe two to three times in one year, charging great up-front fees and paying very little to the leasing company. This genius in Coxson, in understanding human behavior and numbers garnered much respect from a young Bo Baynes (Abu), who had just started out plying his trade in the numbers policy game. Abu told me everyone loved "the maje" in the early days. Hustlers understood the service he was providing, and held no grudge when he needed to recover a vehicle. In those early days Coxson served as both friend and mentor to Abu as well as many young black men looking for a success story in the ghetto.

Sonny Hopson describes his introduction to Major Coxson and their friendship that followed in his book. Hopson, who had a pension for fast cars with a lot of horsepower, who also fashioned himself as a ladies man, was happy to meet the Maje in 1963. According to Hopson, Major was residing in the 5400 block of Angora Terrace, in the Southwest section of Philadelphia, and working for the 46th Street Motors car dealership at 46th & Chestnut Streets, when they met. Major was working as a car salesman and caught Sonny Hopson's eye with a blue Fleetwood Cadillac he drove. Sonny Hopson said he saw Coxson driving through the streets of West Philly in his very distinctive Cadillac. On a visit to Major's place of business, Sonny noticed a Black Coupe De Ville in the display window.

Sonny remembered coming into 46th Street Motors with a pretty woman he was dating named Lois. He introduced himself and his girlfriend to Coxson. He remembered Coxson who was standing in front of him and Lois with a wide grin. Hopson said when Coxson got him alone, he told Hopson that Lois was simply the finest woman he had laid his eyes on in some time. Hopson was only interested in talking about that beautiful black coupe in the window.

According to Hopson, Major said he would do anything for him if he were to pass along Lois's phone number, with the assurance that Hopson would stop seeing her romantically. Hopson, who considered himself pretty capable in the acquisition of women, jumped at the opportunity to trade up his relationship with Lois for the Coupe De Ville. So according to Hopson, the deal had been hatched. Major was separated from his wife, who was the mother of his then ten year old daughter Rhonda, facilitated the purchase of the Coupe DeVille for Hopson in exchange for Lois Luby's phone number. Lois had three young children of her own, and according to many, Coxson and Lois Luby became inseparable. Their dating graduated to sharing a home, which would last until June 8, 1973, the last day of Major Coxson's life.

Major Coxson's first brush with the law happened only three years after he graduated as class president from Benjamin Franklin high school in 1946. These were minor charges of fraud and larceny, which often resulted in suspended sentences. From 1949 to 1967, Coxson was convicted 10 times out of his 17 arrests. In fact, the only serious charge of larceny involved a car theft ring and brought jail time to Coxson. He spent twenty-two months in federal prison at Lewisburg for the offense.

Coxson seemed to have made the best of his time at Lewisburg. It was said that he made connections with members of three of the five Italian crime families controlling New York and all of La Cosa Nostra (Gambino, Genovese and Lucchese), as well as the Bruno crime family in Philadelphia. Coxson was known to boast on the cell block to Mafioso types about his high school friendship with Nicodemo Scarfo, and how he and Nicky banned together against insults about their height.

Prior to 1967, Coxson seemed impervious to his criminal record, but the events of 1967 served as motivation for him to change the way in which he was being perceived. Coxson's role as "citizen" would undergo a serious makeover, but not before facing a serious criminal challenge, as the year's end brought about the man who would serve to inspire Coxson for the last six years of his life, and lead him to heights he would have never imagined for himself.

Coxson drove to Miami in 1964 to watch the boxing match between Sonny Liston, who had resided in Philadelphia for some years prior to the fight, and a young boisterous Cassius Clay. Clay in his own words "shook up the world" with his win against Liston, and soon after announced his conversion to Islam, becoming Muhammad Ali. No one knows for sure if Major met the young champ while in Miami in 1964, but it can be argued that Ali left a lasting impression on Coxson, and by 1967 he would intentionally woo Ali into an unlikely friendship, which some believed led to his undoing. The alliance between Ali and Coxson started with a love of the finer things in life for the two; luxury automobiles, fine Italian suits and women. It started with materialism, but hit its plateau with ideas of changing the Black community through philanthropy and service. It was clear to anyone who knew "the Maj," that he was not only elated about his friendship with Ali, but also determined to cultivate a relationship with Ali which would produce something more than a material change, but that of a transformation into something greater. Unfortunately for Coxson, something not so funny happened on the way to this transformational interaction with Ali, he was indicted.

In the fall of 1967, Major Coxson was listed on a 519 count indictment along with business associates Richard Behrman and Harold Gelvan. An employee of Coxson's, Count Kelly was also listed on the indictment. The indictment came from the New York borough of the Bronx. Richard Behrman and Harold Gelvan advertised high quality automobiles at cut rate prices, but delivered reconditioned taxis and unusable police cars from previous demolitions, or they delivered nothing at all. Behrman and Gelvan operated their "flim-flam" company under the name of Consolidated Auto Wholesalers Inc, apparently scamming customers wasn't new for Richard Behrman. Prior to the 519 count indictment, Behrman had served forty-eight months of a sixty month sentence in Sing Sing prison for substituting parcels of hosiery he promised to customers with old newspapers. Behrman had been released from Sing Sing in 1952.

Apparently the scam was twofold, in that it involved automobiles Behrman's company purchased from Coxson's company, Continental Auto Wholesalers. Behrman's check to Coxson in what were fictitious vehicles, in the amount of $23,750 bounced at a Darby, PA check cashing agency, used by Coxson and owned by an elderly couple left holding the bag for the full amount of the bad check. At the time of their arrest for the check kiting scheme, both Coxson and his employee Count Kelly listed their address as 5400 of Angora Terrace, in Southwest Philadelphia. They were both held in a Philadelphia jail with the prosecutor's goal of extradition to New York. During his legal "cat and mouse" moves with the Bronx District Attorney's Office in the spring of 1968, Coxson had gotten wind of a deal cut between Richard Behrman who sat atop of the 519 count indictment as the "ring-leader," and the prosecutor.

On Thursday, April 11th 1968, Richard Behrman and his companion, 36 year old Mildred Pivnick were murdered in a room above a Millburn, New Jersey art gallery owned by Behrman. Behrman's previous address was 969 Park Avenue, in Manhattan New York, but the indictment had reduced him to consolidating his gallery to a living space. Behrman, a heavy set balding man, had been found seated against the wall of a desk in the gallery's office, shot once in the back of the head. Behrman's companion Marilyn Pivnick, a slender woman neatly dressed in a white checkered suit, was found on the second floor stairway leading to Behrman's office, shot once in the forehead. New Jersey's major crime unit deduced that Behrman was killed first with a 32 caliber pistol, and Pivnick was killed as she came to investigate the noise from the shot which killed Behrman in the office. April 11th was Behrman's 44th and last birthday. Coincidentally, Major Coxson too would die at 44, just twelve days shy of his 45th birthday.

The murders stumped the local authorities, who found themselves without a motive or a murder weapon. The bodies of Behrman and Pivnick were found on the morning of Friday, April 12th by a young part time employee, who traveled from Philadelphia to work at the art gallery. Renwick Mitchell, a protégé of Major Coxson, and future driver of Muhammad Ali was the employee who found the bodies of Coxson's former business associate who decided to testify against him, and the associate's companion. I don't know if law enforcement had known the connection between Renwick Mitchell and Major Coxson at the time of Behrman's murder, or if there were further investigation into the connection.

The Bronx District Attorney's Office suspected Coxson's involvement in Richard Behrman's murder, but had no jurisdiction to investigate the case. On the eve of a major boxing match during the spring of 1973, Muhammad Ali gave a "shout out" to Major Coxson on the Johnny Carson late night variety show, and a special "shout out" to his young driver and friend, Renwick Mitchell, giving credit to Coxson for providing Mitchell as a driver and friend. At the time of Coxson's death, the case in the Bronx against him and Count Kelly was still pending. Harold Gelvan had pleaded guilty to the scam, receiving five years of probation for his cooperation against the remaining conspirators, Count Kelly and Major Coxson. Gelvan went on to start a Disposable Company in New Jersey (NOSAJ), he died in 2013 at the ripe old age of 84.

As for Renwick Mitchell, it seemed his years as a protégé to Coxson were well spent. In February 1988, almost 15 years after Major Coxson's death, Renwick Mitchell was indicted for laundering money for drug dealers through a car dealership, where he worked as a salesman of high end luxury cars, in a suburb near Philadelphia.

Along with Coxson's budding friendship with Ali in 1967, his best friend and business associate Stanley Branche had entered into the arena of politics, as he ran for the mayor of Chester, PA. Many believed Coxson's relationship with both Ali and Branche changed his goals towards real legitimacy, and may have also taken him to desperate measures in protection of those new goals.

In the streets, a "balloon" refers to a package of heroin, in business jargon a "balloon payment" refers to a large or enormous final payment which must be paid before a debt is settled. In March of 1973, Bo Baynes (Abu) was expecting a large heroin package worth one million dollars on the street. The package was sent from a New York dealer affiliated with the Genovese crime family. Not soon after Abu had received an expected time of arrival on the delivery, had he received the news that the package had been intercepted.

Major Coxson seemed to be in full throttle of his mayoral campaign that spring. Even his good friend Muhammad Ali had committed himself to helping Coxson win the election, through his lending of luxury vehicles to Coxson, and free television advertisement through shout outs. Coxson must have been a master multi-tasker, as with everything a mayoral candidate would have to do in the last thirty days of a primary election, he also took time to respond to the streets.

According to law enforcement, Coxson was apparently summoned to a meeting in April by someone in the Genovese crime family. No one knows the actual conversation of the meeting between Coxson and the New York Mafioso figure, but what has been speculated has become legend. Coxson is thought to have made a six figure deal to recover the package slated for Abu. Upon recovery of the one million dollar package, Coxson was to receive $300,000 for his trouble. Since the package hadn't arrived for Abu, he wasn't on the hook for its cost, nor was he responsible for its retrieval, but clearly he had a horse in the race.

Knowing he had no time to do the investigating required to find the package himself, Coxson is thought to have sub-contracted out his deal with the New York folks for the retrieval of the package, without divulging what he was being paid to locate the balloons. He was heard offering $200,000 for the "uncut" delivery of the heroin, which would allow him to keep $100,000 of the stake for himself. Just before the primary election occurred, the bullet torn bodies of Hilton Stroud and Walter Tillman were found on May 1st in Camden, New Jersey.

It's been widely accepted that it was Stroud and Tillman who intercepted the heroin package by hijacking the vehicle used by the drug carrier. What was speculated in the press after Coxson's murder was the possibility that he had ordered the hit on Stroud and Tillman. What the press did not know of was the sub-contract for the recovery of the package, what they also didn't know was who actually bought the contract.

According to insiders, the Black mafia, the same group who lost the package had taken on Coxson's bet to retrieve it. In most sectors of business, this would qualify as a "conflict of interest," why the conflict hadn't occurred to Coxson suggests he was either preoccupied with the election or he failed to do his due diligence. What was also unknown to both law enforcement and the media, was the notion that most local dealers and stick up artists alike knew better than to steal from the Black mafia, they knew the consequence would mean sudden death.

Many believe Stroud and Tillman had no idea the package was destined for Bo Baynes. Coxson was known to have a connection to Frank Matthews, who at the time was the largest heroin distributor on the eastern seaboard. It was believed that Coxson would screen dealers for Frank, receiving a large fee. After Coxson's death, an informant told law enforcement that Coxson would meet dealers in hotels, checking to see if they had the initial financials for the buy before sending them to Frank Matthews.

Frank Matthews was originally from North Carolina, but had spent his teenage years in the city of brotherly love. Like Bo Baynes and Major Coxson, Frank had been involved in the numbers policy business in Philadelphia. The numbers game may have been too much of a slow grind for Matthews, as he soon graduated into heroin distribution once he moved to New York. By the time the Black mafia had convened its first meeting in 1968, Matthews operation had become a well-oiled machine, with links to major drug dealers within the Philadelphia corridor. John "Pops" Darby was a major player in the Frank Matthews operation, alongside a young dealer by the name of Tyrone Palmer, also known affectionately as "Mr. Millionaire," due to his association with Frank Matthews.

Tyrone Palmer was murdered inside Club Harlem in Atlantic City, New Jersey on Easter Sunday 1972, according to law enforcement, members of the Black mafia murdered Tyrone Palmer, and they murdered him because of a refusal on the part of Frank Matthews to pay tribute to the mafia for doing business in Philly.

In late January 1973, Frank Matthews had been arrested in Nevada and held before being extradited to New York for a major RICO trial. The word had gotten out about Matthews arrest and upcoming trial, so many believe the hijackers thought the heroin belonged to Matthews and believed they were catching him in a vulnerable position due to the recent arrest. Coincidentally, Frank Matthews disappeared in late June 1973, only two weeks after Coxson's murder. Frank Matthews is believed to have left the country with more than twenty million dollars, he was never heard from again.

Another thread to this narrative is the belief that Coxson actually had a meeting with New York Mafioso members before the hijacking that may have precipitated the robbery. The belief is that Coxson was followed up to New York by Stroud and Tillman during the first meeting and were able to create a trail on the "family's drug courier." So Coxson may have been called back in to retrieve the package because some may have blamed him for the courier's route being exposed.

An average person given an ultimatum to gather two hundred thousand dollars within forty-eight hours would have taken their family, money and passport to get as far away from the threat as possible, not so for Major Coxson. Even though he was unable to recover the package of heroin Stroud and Tillman are believed to have stolen from a courier, Coxson was still on the hook for the promised $200,000 he subcontracted out to the Black mafia.

According to newspaper articles at the time of his death, Coxson was seen with Muhammad Ali on the afternoon of June 7th, a day before his death, which indicated to some that Major may have been trying to gather the funds. The heavyweight champion had supported Coxson's political campaign in Camden, even to the point of doing photo opportunities for Coxson in the last days of the primary election. Ali even talked about his friendship with Coxson on radio and television interviews, often quoting "The Maj," which made Ali's comments after learning of Coxson's death all the more curious. Ali was quoted to have said, "My hands are clean. I am a Muslim and I believe in Allah, and Allah will take care of me because my hands are clean." In Ali's defense, we don't know what he was asked in respect to Major Coxson to prompt the statement.

Also on Thursday, June 7th around noon, Major received a young man named Jim Walton and his father in law. Jim, who was around twenty five years of age had taken a liking to the flashy nouveau politician. Jim was himself an aspiring wheeler dealer, who would make in excess of a million dollars some twenty years later, securing financing for churches looking to go mega. Coxson was equally impressed with young Jim Walton, providing him and his father in law with a "nickel" tour of his renovated "white house" in Camden, also respecting Walton enough not to hit him up for a loan, which seemed futile at this point.

About 3:00 p.m., Coxson was back in Philadelphia. Apparently he was attempting to make one last ditch effort to raise the funds. He reportedly visited South Philly bookies connected with the Bruno crime family. Frank "Chickie" Narducci and Frank Sindone were bookies/loan sharks known to hustlers and law enforcement alike. It was reported that Coxson had visited both Franks, to no avail. His relationship with the Philadelphia branch of La Cosa Nostra seemed to have cooled. Coxson had served time with wise guys in Lewisburg for his fraud conviction, and had proven himself useful in securing vehicles for the mob as well as their associates, when requested. Coxson's old high school buddy couldn't be of any use to him either.

Nicky Scarfo was sharing a house with his mother and cousin Phillip "Crazy Phil" Leonetti in Atlantic City, during Coxson's last quest for assistance. Scarfo had been banished to Atlantic City some ten years earlier, due to a brawl at a South Philly diner over a booth which left a longshoreman dead. Scarfo, who had been made a member of La Cosa Nostra in 1954, had been charged and convicted of manslaughter.

According to sources, the newly installed "Docile Don," Angelo Bruno, was not happy with Scarfo's sporadic temper causing the death of a citizen, and bringing unnecessary attention to the family. So after Scarfo's release from prison for the manslaughter beef, Don Bruno sent him to Atlantic City to ply his trade in loan sharking and bookmaking. Mind you, this relocation to Atlantic City predates the arrival of the casinos, which didn't arrive until 1976. Scarfo was stuck in a virtual wasteland, one of the worst punishments for earners. Although Scarfo couldn't have been any help to Coxson financially in his hour of need, Coxson was planning to take a trip to Atlantic City with two of his closest friends from Philadelphia on Friday, June 8th.

About 5:00 p.m., on Thursday June 7th, Coxson spent time with his dear friends Gus Lacey and Stanley Branche, out of Branche's center city office for his company, Advance Security at 1405 Locust Street. Branche and Coxson were former partners of the Rolls Royce Supper Club, located in the 200 block of South Broad Street. Coxson eventually bought Branche's interest before reselling the popular night spot to Lillian Reis, girlfriend of a La Cosa Nostra associate. Reis, notorious in her own right for an underworld heist which netted her more than a half million dollars in the early 1960's.

Coxson was following the successful formula with the Rolls Royce Club laid out for him by his great friend Gus Lacey. Lacey was proprietor of Mr. Silk's Third Base, an upscale club on the 52nd Street corridor. Lacey had served the likes of Lena Horne, Billy Eckstein and Sammy Davis whenever they were in town. Both Branche and Lacey told the authorities they had been with Coxson in Branche's office, chatting it up until about 8:00 p.m. on the evening of June 7th. Both also said Coxson didn't appear to have a care in the world. Coxson was described as being his jovial and carefree self. According to Branche and Lacey, Coxson left the office saying that he had to get dressed for a dinner engagement, and committed to joining them in Atlantic City for the following evening.

Those interviewing Branche and Lacey asked if Coxson had sought physical protection. Branched stated that if he were seeking protection, he would have come to him, especially since Branche owned a detective agency. Branche and Lacey appeared to be Coxson's last stop before heading back to Cherry Hill for what became his last night alive.

According to reports, the carnage at 1146A Barbara Drive began at 4:00 a.m., as thirteen year old Lex Luby, son of Coxson's common law wife Lois told police he and the entire family were awakened by the sound of a car's horn honking in the driveway. The honking horn brought Coxson to the foyer to see who was in the driveway, Lex reporting to hear a muffled voice calling to Coxson and his response "I'm coming Sam." The noise reportedly brought Lois Luby to the foyer as well. Coxson reportedly told Lois to go back to bed as he welcomed four Black men into the living room. The initial conversation seemed to be cordial and friendly before morphing into a loud verbal confrontation. All five residents, including Major Coxson were bound and gagged. Coxson was taken to his bedroom where he was shot, once in the back of the head. Lois and her two children, Lita and Toro were also shot. Major

Coxson and Lita Luby's shots were fatal. Lois and Toro survived the shootings, but were both blinded. Lex managed to slip out of the wrappings used to bind him. He slipped out of the glass sliding door and ran down the street to Mrs. Zehair Khalil's house, she let Toro inside and notified the authorities.

Major Coxson had been known to say to anyone listening, "with the life I've led, If anyone cries at my funeral, I want you to run them out." As much as his loved ones wanted to honor his wishes, many fell short. The "Maj" was laid to rest on Friday, June 15th 1973, just one week after the bloody event in Cherry Hill. His funeral was held at the Wayland Baptist Church, at 25th & Columbia Avenue in North Philadelphia (the avenue is now Cecil B. Moore Avenue, after Major Coxson and Stanley Branche's friend).
Wayland Baptist was the home church of the Reverend Clarence Smith, who was its pastor up until May of 1970 when he was murdered in his home. Clarence Fowler, also known as Sham-Sudin Ali, was convicted of killing Rev. Smith, the conviction was later overturned on appeal.

Five thousand people came to the church for "the Maj's" final home going. Many had confessed that they were actually hoping to catch a glimpse of Muhammad Ali, who didn't attend the funeral but sent a five foot high bouquet of chrysanthemums and red carnations, with a caption reading "Dear friend." Local radio host Mary Mason, an old friend of Coxson, served as the mistress of ceremonies at the funeral.

The procession was ripe with drama from the start, as police had to close the church during the funeral due to a bomb threat. A police helicopter was also hovering over the neighborhood, contributing to the already noisy procession. Major Coxson was laid out to rest in an ebony steel casket, wearing a black suit with a white shirt and a black and red print tie. He wore black leather shoe boots, called "celebrity boots," as they were popular with entertainers of the era. There was also a white fedora lying in the coffin near Coxson's head. A satin stream lay next to the coffin with the words "We love you Major."

Coxson's father Israel, a deacon at Wayland Baptist, was said to let out a big gasp upon viewing the body. Coxson's older brother Israel Jr. fainted during the procession, and was taken to a back room in the church to be revived. There were many speakers at Coxson's funeral. A lifelong friend named Dr. Frederick Bryant spoke of his friend's potential in other areas of life. He said, "May I remind the white structure that here is a man who could have stood with the world's financial geniuses if he had been given the opportunity to do so." Coxson was also eulogized by F.

Emmett Fitzpatrick, his lawyer and the then democratic candidate for Philadelphia's
District Attorney Office.

In great irony, Fitzpatrick who went on to win the general election in the fall of
1973, would go on to prosecute many of the cases involving Coxson's associates years
later, including those suspected of killing him. Fitzpatrick spoke of Major's love of
life, as if he knew him well. I suspect Mr. Fitzpatrick saw a great opportunity to fish
for votes.

Coxson was buried at the Mount Lawn Cemetery in Sharon Hill, Delaware County, right
outside of Philadelphia. There was said to have been more than fifty cars in the
funeral procession, with the belief that for every luxury car in the procession, there
was at least one law enforcement agent in the car that followed. Major Coxson's
twenty four year old daughter Rhonda, from his marriage with his estranged wife
Elizabeth, was so distraught at the burial site, she needed to be restrained, while
Coxson's parents were aided in their bereavement at his final resting place.

A prevailing theory on the strong presence of law enforcement at Coxson's funeral
and burial is the belief that perpetrators may have also been in attendance. Law
enforcement soon learned that there were as many motives for Major Coxson's
untimely demise as those attending his home going.

In the F.B.I. file on the Black mafia, there are at least a half dozen reasons given for
Coxson's demise. Most of the information gathered by the F.B.I. was acquired by the
way of informants. One informant apparently reported to the feds that four men had
come to Coxson's house on June 8th about money owed them for two shows they'd
helped Coxson put on at the Latin Casino. The informant identified the assailants as
Black Muslims, and added that the Muslims had worked as ticket takers as well as
security, but either didn't get paid by Coxson, or thought they'd deserved a larger
amount of the take. The informant described the discussion between Coxson and the
four assailants as civil in the beginning, with Coxson sitting in his living room and
explaining that he had no cash, but telling the four they were free to take his watch
and close circuit television system, worth several thousand dollars. According to the
informant, voices were raised and the conversation escalated into a pistol whipping
for Coxson that ultimately led to his and Lita Luby's murder. The informant claimed,
prior to hearing of Coxson's death, he overheard one of the assailants saying if
Muslims received no money from the 2nd show, Coxson would breathe his last breath.

Another informant eluded to the possibility that Coxson had been set up by someone in his inner circle. Coxson was known to have a bodyguard with him at all times, even to have his bodyguard occupy space in his home while he slept. The informant noted that the bodyguard wasn't present during Coxson's assault and subsequent murder, leading to the possibility that Coxson was set up by his bodyguard. Yet another informant totally discounted any notion of Coxson being involved in narcotics deals, thus stating the murder had nothing to do with drugs. This informant stated that Coxson had borrowed a great sum of money to finance his campaign, from a loan shark with mafia connections (It wasn't stated whether the mafia connections were Italian or Black). The informant went on to state Coxson had not only promised to pay back the principle amount of the loan, but deliver the city of Camden to the loan shark for business. So the story goes, when Coxson lost the primary election, not only was he unable to deliver the city to the loan shark, but he had also lost the ability to repay the loan. So, following the informant's logic, Coxson was executed for his failure to deliver Camden and repay the debt.

Based on much of the informant's information, law enforcement and the media ran with the motive of Coxson being killed due to his reneging of payment on a contract to kill Hilton Stroud and Walter Tillman. Both Stroud and Tillman had been murdered only a month before Coxson, in Camden. Law enforcement were running with a theory of a drug war with Stroud and Tillman in the middle of the war with the Black mafia. Stroud and Tillman were suspects in the multiple shooting of Black mafia co-founder Donnie Day. On the street, it was widely believed that Coxson subcontracted the retrieval of the package out to the same guys embittered in a war with Stroud and Tillman. Stroud and Tillman were believed to have been murdered before the whereabouts of the package were ascertained.

During my visit to Abu's for the summit meeting in 2008, I took the opportunity to ask Donny Day about Major Coxson. Since the case was considered closed at this point, I thought no harm could be attached to my question, nor was I attempting to use it in a way that would incriminate anyone. I flat out asked opinions on why Major Coxson was killed? I was flabbergasted by the response. After some silence, Day mentioned "testosterone" as a major factor. The belief that there were some in the group who had more "alpha" than others, and their constant need to demonstrate. Another founding member shook his head in agreement, stating that the member who was convicted of killing Coxson (Ronald Harvey Sr.) was always trying to "one up" him, and so when he participated in events it would get out of hand on occasion based on that factor. I asked if Ali was a factor in Coxson becoming a target, and through the silence and nods I received somewhat of a confirmation. Another founding associate nodded to me and said, "yeah, there was some animosity in the way Major had attached himself to our brother because those of us who knew em, felt like he was using Ali for his own gain." I knew enough at that point to quit while I was ahead, so I didn't ask any questions related to hijacked heroin packages, or subcontracts going south, as I knew I would be traveling into risky territory, even with these now "lovable old rouges." However, what I was able to find in my research served to put the puzzle of Coxson's death together with what the founding members were able to contribute.

The article's title "The Mayor's dream house," referenced a $200,000 bid on a property being built for Frank Rizzo, then mayor of Philadelphia by Muhammad Ali and Major Coxson. The article suggested that Ali and Coxson were collaborating to buy the property out from under the feet of Frank Rizzo, but more than that, the article suggested a real partnership between Ali and Coxson and that both had money. The article ran in the Chicago paper just 6 days before Coxson's murder. I think the news article on Ali and Coxson in their bid for the Rizzo house, as well as an additional magazine article on Coxson, which profiled his glamorous life in Cherry Hill and beautiful family provided a "perfect storm" for those with an ax to grind, to act on June 8th as they did. I also believe there was some drinking and perhaps some drugging occurring prior to the trip to Coxson's Cherry Hill house, on that fateful morning. I believe the drugs and testosterone got the better of everyone involved, and with that, the lives of Major Coxson and Lita Luby were taken. I believe the trip was fueled by the desperation of those who were dealing with the heat of law enforcement at the time, which had an enormous effect on their money flow, coupled with advertised "bromance" exasperated the jealousy of Coxson's friendship to Ali.

CHAPTER SEVEN

Seeds of a Hypocrite

On Tuesday, April 25th, 1973, Sarah Robinson called her supervisor at the downtown motel to inform him that she'd be taking a day off due to recurring back pain. Sarah, who was forty-five years old, worked as a chambermaid at the motel. She had had spells of chronic back pain since she was in her early twenties. Sarah had planned to get a few more hours of rest before she went to pay a visit to her chiropractor. At about 10:30 that morning, Sarah's plan to rest was interrupted by a knock at the door. Upon opening her front door, Sarah wished she had gone to work instead.

Detectives Branson and Jacobs stepped into the corridor of Sarah Robinson's house to inform her that they would need her to appear at a line-up on May 3rd, to identify some of the eight black men who stayed at the motel on January 17th. Sarah was on duty the 17th of January, the eve of the Hanafi massacre. She had seen and had even given one of the men a towel. Detective Jacobs had interviewed Sarah Robinson on January 24th. They had taken her statement, and informed her that they would need her to attend a line-up at a later date to possibly identify some of the suspects. Since the interview Sarah Robinson had wished that she hadn't worked at all that day.

Sarah had been reading the newspaper accounts of the murders. The newspapers were calling the murders a religious war between Muslim factions. They also insinuated that the murders were a contract killing, planned by the powerful leaders of the Nation of Islam. Sarah thought to herself, "I'm just a middle-aged chambermaid working in a fleabag motel." Sarah didn't want the responsibility that came with identifying someone accused of committing such a heinous act. She thought that if these men could kill babies who couldn't identify anyone, then they wouldn't think twice about killing a middle-aged woman that could help put them away.

Sensing a bit of reluctance from Sarah Robinson, Detective Jacobs assured her that no one would know her identity until the trial, and if necessary the police would move Ms.

Robinson out of the area until the trial began. This made Sarah Robinson feel a little safer, so she agreed to attend the line-up on May 3ʳᵈ.

The next morning, Detectives Branson and Jacobs boarded the metro-liner train to Philadelphia. They arrived in Philadelphia at 11:00 o'clock that morning, and went directly to the Philadelphia Police department's homicide unit. They were in town to serve subpoenas on six of the eight suspects in the case. Detectives Branson and Jacobs were armed with their subpoenas signed by a federal magistrate presiding over the grand jury investigation into the murders. Although they had federal subpoenas in their possession, they still needed the assistance of the local law enforcement to execute the process.

Philadelphia homicide detectives did the legwork in finding the suspects for Detective Branson and Jacobs. Four of the six subpoenaed for the line-up were already in police custody for other offenses. The crime binge that followed the Hanafi murders resulted in detainment for John Clark, Jerome Sinclair, Theodore Moody, and James Price. James Price was incarcerated only a day before Branson and Jacob's arrival.

Price was being held on the Baldwin Dairies holdup in Frankford, and also for the robbery-murder of Myer Abrams at his junkyard on April 6ᵗʰ. Theodore Moody was identified as a suspect in a mass rape and robbery that occurred in early January in North Philadelphia.

A birthday party was held at a house in North Philadelphia, when four men burst in with guns. The men tied-up everyone in the house then robbed them. They also stripped several women in the house and raped them. A .38 caliber pistol was stolen in the robbery, which was later identified by Washington D.C. ballistics' team as being the pistol left at the Hanafi crime scene. Theodore Moody had been held at Philadelphia's detention center since February 12ᵗʰ.

Four days earlier, John Clark, Williams Christian, John Griffin, and a fourth man named Richard Dabney forced their way into the home of Ernest Kelly, and held his family hostage while Clark escorted Kelly to the bank to withdraw $100,000 dollars. Of course their plot failed miserably, and Christian, Dabney, and Griffin were arrested for kidnapping. Clark had fled the scene, but was picked up by the FBI on March 16ᵗʰ and charged with bank robber and kidnapping.

Jerome Sinclair, the suspect in the Yellow Cab hold-up who had managed to free Christian and Griffin by posting their bail in February, was himself arrested and charged with the Yellow Cab robbery a week later. Since four of the six were already in custody, Detectives Branson and Jacobs needed an extradition order signed by a federal judge, to take the prisoners to Washington for a line-up.

They quickly got a judge to sign off on the order to extradite the suspects and were on their way to serve the two remaining suspects, William Christian and John Griffin. Philadelphia's homicide detectives retrieved the addresses of William Christian and John Griffin for the detectives, who were deciding how to make the server leave a strong impact on the suspects. Detective Branson had mentioned splitting up to serve the suspects. They had two of

Philadelphia's homicide detectives escort both him and Jacobs to the suspects residences. Branson thought that it would be more powerful to serve both Christian and Griffin simultaneously, thus not giving either the opportunity to warn the other. Detective Jacobs and the Philadelphia detectives decided against Detective Branson's suggestion. They thought it would be more powerful if each suspect opened his door to find four homicide dicks standing out in front with a federal subpoena. The detectives' first trip was to William Christian's house.

William Christian resided on the 2700 block of Newkirk Street, in North Philadelphia, with his wife and two daughters. At 1:00 o'clock that afternoon, the four detectives stood in front of William Christian's house. Detective Jacobs knocked on William Christian's door with his right hand as he held the subpoena with his left. A tall black man wearing gray slacks and a navy blue shirt opened the door. The detectives asked him if he was William Christian, and he responded in the affirmative. Then, Detective Jacobs handed William Christian the federal subpoena and informed him that he was required to appear in Washington D.C. on May 3, 1973 for a line-up. William Christian appeared to be visibly nervous, and asked Detective Jacobs, what if I'm picked? Detective Jacobs responded, "If you're picked, then there's a great possibility that you will be indicted by the grand jury and held for trial." With his head facing the ground, William Christian said, thank you, took the subpoena and closed the door. Their next trip was to 1424 Tioga Street, the home of John Griffin.

John Griffin, who like Christian, was out of jail on bail for the Kelly kidnapping, was also facing parole violations for the weapons' charge. As detectives reached John Griffin's door, a tall, thin dark skinned male walked out of an adjacent door. Detective Branson walked up to the man and asked him for identification. The man said, "Yes, I'm John Griffin. What do you want?" Detective Jacobs said, "We want you in Washington D.C. on May 3, 1973, to appear in a line-up as a suspect in the Hanafi murders." Then he handed John Griffin his subpoena, and asked him if he had any questions. John Griffin staring hard at the detective said, no, not at this moment. The four detectives departed.

The four suspects being detained received their subpoenas the same day, while Detectives Branson and Jacobs were on their way back to the nation's capital.

On May 3rd, Sarah Robinson, nervous and sleep deprived, walked into Metropolitan police headquarters, escorted by a uniformed officer. Almina Khaalis, Hamaas Khaalis' daughter who was shot several times in the head, was also present for the line-up. An hour earlier, a prison van from Philadelphia pulled up to the prisoner's entrance of the Metropolitan police building. Four men got out of the van wearing Philadelphia prison uniforms. The four men were John Clark, Jerome Sinclair, Theodore Moody, and James Price.

The line-up began promptly at 10:00 o'clock in the morning. William Christian and John Griffin had obviously decided to ignore the subpoena requiring their appearance. Detective Branson put four local criminals with similar height and complexion into the line-up with the four suspects.

As Sarah Robinson studied the profile of each suspect, the evening of January 17th invaded her thoughts. She remembered a dark skinned gentlemen, who stood about five feet eleven inches, with a big forehead, big lips and a broad nose asking her for an extra towel. She studied each suspect, looking for those attributes. Only one suspect, Jerome Sinclair had most of the attributes of the man Sarah Robinson spoke to in the hallway of the motel. Jerome Sinclair had a broad nose, and big lips, but he didn't have a big forehead.

Sarah Robinson told Detectives Branson, "Number six resembles the man, I talked to the most, but he's not him, the man had a larger forehead." Detective Branson took Sarah Robinson out of the line-up room and into his office to look at pictures.

Detective Branson had secured the mugshots of William Christian and John Griffin in case they failed to appear for the line-up. He showed her ten pictures, both Christian's and Griffin's pictures with eight local criminals. Sarah Robinson looked intently at each picture, and then she shouts, "It's him!" Detective Branson looked at Sarah Robinson and smiled. He said, "Thank you very much for your cooperation. You can go now. We will be in touch when the grand jury convenes."

Sarah Robinson identified William Christian's picture as the man who asked her for a towel at the motel on January 17th. Unlike Sarah Robinson, who was very nervous about identifying the murder suspects, Almina Khaalis walked into the police station confidently, with the intent to identify her family's killers.

When the light came on and the eight suspects stood there on stage, a tear trickled down Almina's face. Detective Jacobs asked her if she would be alright to do the identifications. She confidently said, yes, don't mind my tears, they are tears of anger in having to be in close proximity to these animals, and not be able to do anything to them. Almina flagged the first four suspects, who were local criminals. When she got a glance at number five, she said he looks a lot like the leader. The leader was tall, slender, and light skinned, without facial hair or glasses. She repeated herself, he looks a lot like the leader, but I don't know if I can make a positive identification.

John Clark was suspect number five. Almina looked intently at six and seven, but couldn't identify either one as being the perpetrators. Almina had continued to say since the day of the carnage, that all of the men involved in the murders of her family, she would always remember the face of the man who took her baby from her arms.

When Almina got a look at the eighth suspect, she raised her arms above her head, as to relive the event when her daughter was taken. She said, "That's him, number eight, that's the one who took my baby from me. That's him!" Almina positively identified James Price as one of the men who came to her house to rob and murder the Khaalis family.

The entire investigation team was salivating over this victory. They knew now who to target as a weak link, the same man who gave their investigator the names of his co-conspirators, no other than James H. Price.

On May 7th, Detectives Branson and Jacobs, returned to Philadelphia to kill three birds with one stone. The first two birds were William Christian, and John Griffin. The stone was a warrant for their arrest for their failure to appear in Washington for the May 3rd line-up. Accompanied by Philadelphia's finest, Detectives Branson and Jacobs decided to split up this time, so that they could arrest Christian and Griffin simultaneously.

At noon, both detectives were knocking on the doors of Christian and Griffin to no avail. Detective Jacobs suspected that both Christian and Griffin flew the coop, so he had the Philadelphia police department put out an "all points bulletin" on Christian and Griffin, and leak their status as wanted fugitives to the media.

Their last bird to kill was James Price. Price had been brought back to Philadelphia after the line-up, to await trial for the murder of Myer Abrams.

Detective Branson went to the detention center where James Price was being held to have him released into his custody for interrogation. At 2:00 p.m. an officer from the sheriff's department escorted Price to the interrogation room at police headquarters. Price knew the room well. He remembered the interrogation he had there a month earlier about Myer Abram's murder. He also remembered his first interrogation he had there four years ago, when at nineteen, he was charged with the robbery-murder of Ben Ami.

Price had a sinister grin on his face, as he walked into the interrogation room. Detectives Branson and Jacobs introduced themselves, and informed Price of his rights. Detective Jacobs then began to tell Price of the evidence they had amassed against him. He said, "James, we're not here to bullshit you. It looks pretty bad for you. We haven't gotten as much evidence on anyone else yet, but we definitely got you." Price, still grinning, said, "You ain't got shit, until one of us talks! You ain't got shit!" Repeating himself, Jacob says, "We've got you, Price, we've got you."

Price responded, "Okay, I'll play along. What do you have?" he says, animating his voice as if to be performing a minstrel. Detective Jacobs, now grinning, told Price that they have a witness identification of him at the scene, they have phone records from the motel of a collect call made to his house, and they have the statement from a witness that Price implicated himself in the murders along with seven others.

After Detective Jacobs made the last statement, Price's grin turned into a grimace. Price's whole demeanor changed. Price said, "What the hell do you mean about a statement of me incriminating myself and seven others?" As soon as Price finished the statement, Remus Williams walked into the interrogation room. Detective Branson, now grinning, also said, "Oh, Mr. Price, please allow me to introduce you to detective Williams."

Price's eye almost popped out of his head, as he became increasingly nervous. He said, "I don't believe this shit, Remus, you fucking rat." Remus stared at Price without blinking, and said, "You're a child murderer, and you have the nerve to call me a rat. If you weren't in custody, I'd kick your ass!"

Price began shaking, he said, "You don't understand what kind of position you put me in, you just signed my death warrant." Detective Branson told Price to calm down. He told Price that at the moment, he was only looking at seven counts of second-degree murder, since the victims were not the intended targets.

Detective Branson told Price, "If you cooperate with us, give us something more to go to the grand jury with, then we will allow you to plea this out to three counts of manslaughter." Price replied, "You're just a detective, how in the hell can you guarantee something like that?" Detective Branson informed James Price that one of the federal prosecutors trying the case was in the next room, and would speak with him as soon as he agreed to the deal. Price then asked to see the prosecutor and said that he might agree after talking with the prosecutor. Detective Branson immediately got on the phone. He said, "Mr. Evans, he would like to speak with you before making a deal, can you join us?"

John Evans, the U.S. assistant attorney, was one of the federal prosecutors assigned to take the Hanafi case to the grand jury. Mr. Evans walked into the interrogation room, and James Price, without introduction said, "Can you guarantee a manslaughter charge?" Mr. Evans said, "Yes, I can, James. Are you ready to tell us what happened?" Price said, "Alright, what do you want to know?"

Detective Branson said, "First of all, we want to know the rationale of the killings." Price replied, "You mean you want to know why we killed them?" Detective Branson said, "Yes." Price continued, "I think you know why, because of the letter." Detective Jacobs said, "That's what I figured, but we needed to hear you say it." Detective Branson interjected," "Before we go any further James, we need to know who ordered the murders." James Price becoming agitated said, "Let me tell you this now so that I won't have to say it again, I will only give you what I mistakenly gave your detective Remus, only the guys who did the murders, If you want the person at the top, you've got to shake the tree a little harder." Detective Jacobs said, "Very well then, let's get back to the murders. We're under the assumption that your only target on January 18ᵗʰ was Hamaas Khaalis." Price shook his head, affirming the statement. Detective Jacobs continued, he said, "Did you all have a contingency plan set up in case Mr. Khaalis was not at home?" Price said, "No, we were doing this thing under the assumption that we were gonna find him at home and kill him."

Assistant prosecutor Evans then climbed in, he asked Price if it mattered if anyone else was in the house when Mr. Khaalis was to be murdered. Price answered, "No!" Evans seemingly shook and said, "So then the five children and the others were no accident?" Again Price said, "No!" He elaborated, saying that they had decided at a meeting that no witnesses would be left alive. Evans was dumbfounded.

Prior to his confession, he and the investigative team were operating under the assumption that the children's murder was pure happenstance, no premeditation. Evans had to reiterate his question for clarity. He said, "Let me understand what you're saying. Prior to arriving at the house, you all had the knowledge that there were small children in the house, and that you were going to kill them along with Mr. Khaalis and his wife and daughter?" Price responded blankly, "No, we didn't have prior knowledge that they were in the house, but once we discovered that they were there, they had to die with everyone else."

The investigator just looked at Price with a cold stare. Then he asked loudly, "Why didn't you all just lock the kids in the basement or something?" Four of the five kids, who were nine days old to three years old were too young to identify you anyway." Price got angry and said, "You white motherfuckers don't understand. They were expendable because they were the seeds of a hypocrite! The hypocrite disrespected the messenger, and for that punishment is death! Death! Do you understand what this means? We are soldiers for the messengers, soldiers for truth, soldiers for a new Black nation. If you are an enemy of the messenger, then you must die and if you happen to have your wife and kids with you when we decide to take you out, then that's your problem. We don't have any sympathy for the seeds of devils or hypocrites. If you're a seed of hypocrites, then you don't have the potential to become anything but a hypocrite yourself. So all we did was do everyone a favor in the future. Five less hypocrites to deal with at a later date is how I see it."

Evans stated that after James Price finished his soliloquy, they were all left with blank stares. Evans admitted that at least they knew with whom they were dealing, cold-blooded killers. After making his statement, Price struck a deal with the prosecution that would allow him to be tried separately from his co-defendants, where prior to trial he would be allowed to enter a plea of guilty only of conspiracy to commit murder, in return for his cooperation.

When the stenographer finished recording James Price's statement, he signed it. The detectives looked up at the prosecutor Evans. They looked up at him as if to ask if he thought the confession was enough to go back to the grand jury. Mr. Evans looked up at the detectives, nodded and said, "I think we are ready to present our case."

CHAPTER EIGHT
Trial and Error

On July 5, 1973 James Price gave testimony to a grand jury in Washington D.C. He gave testimony about his and other's roles in the Hanafi murders. The U.S. Attorneys Robert Shuker and John Evans felt they had an airtight case. They were confident that a grand jury would indict all eight suspects, after hearing James Price's testimony.

John Clark, Theodore Moody, and Jerome Sinclair were also being held at the detention center for charges on other crimes. William Christian and John Griffin were considered to be fugitives for failing to respond to a federal subpoena, requesting their appearance in Washington for the line-up.

On the very same day that James Price testified in front of a grand jury, Ronald Harvey was being arraigned for the murders of Major Coxson and his step-daughter. Harvey was given bail at the arraignment, with a pre-trial date set for August 17ᵗʰ, 1973.

On August 15, 1973, the grand jury indicted John Clark, William Christian, John Griffin, Ronald Harvey, Theodore Moody, James Price, Jerome Sinclair and an eighth man named Thomas Clinton, whose indictment was made immediately invalid due to his death from leukemia a month earlier. The indictments were headlines in Washington D.C., but in Philadelphia, there was a greater impact.

John Clark, Theodore Moody, James Price and Jerome Sinclair were already in custody, so the extradition for the four would be simple. As for William Christian and John Griffin, the F.B.I. would be brought back into the case to help bring them to justice. Since Ronald Harvey was free on $175,000 bail, and scheduled to appear in court on August 17ᵗʰ, the prosecutors had planned to be present at the hearing with their extradition paper in hand.

Harvey's pretrial hearing was the first case on the courts' dockets that morning. Detectives Branson, Jacobs and Williams waited impatiently in the courtroom corridor for the proceedings to begin. The detectives were savoring the moment. Finally, they were going to tie up their end of the investigation, and pass the baton on to the prosecutors to bring the accused to justice.

At 8:55 a.m. Ronald Harvey's attorney walked into the courthouse. Detective Williams noticed that the usually confident and arrogant counsel looked worried. After studying the defense attorney's body language, Detective Williams turned to the others and said that he thought Harvey had skipped. Detectives Branson and Jacobs also looked at Harvey's attorney for confirmation of William's statement. Both Branson and Jacobs agreed with Williams. Branson got up to call the federal prosecutors, informing them of their fears. As Branson got up, the Bailiff called everyone into the courtroom to begin the hearing.

Detective Jacobs and Williams walked into the courtroom behind the Camden County District Attorney. The presiding judge walked in and proceeded to conduct a roll call. The judge said, "I see the prosecutor, the investigators, and the defense counsel, but we seem to be missing a crucial ingredient in this case. Where's your client counsel?" Harvey's attorney stood to his feet, and told the judge that his secretary had made several unsuccessful attempts to reach Harvey last night, as well as this morning. Appearing to be very annoyed by the defense's revelations, the judge told Harvey's attorney that he will give him approximately five minutes to get his client to the courthouse, front and center. Harvey's attorney simply nodded in agreement.

Suddenly the courtroom door swung open violently, and everyone inside turned around, in anticipation of Ronald Harvey's arrival, but it was only Detective Branson. Looking back at the gazing eyes, he smiled because he realized that they thought he was Ronald Harvey coming into the courtroom.

Branson sat down next to Jacobs and Williams, and whispered to them the details of his phone conversation. He said, "Guys, I just spoke with a friend at the bureau. After I informed him that Harvey possibly skipped bail, he informed me that Harvey will probably be put on their ten most wanted list."

Williams looked at Branson with a grin, then remarked, "You knew all along that Harvey would skip, didn't you?" Branson replied, "I had a hunch, but I figured since he posted seventeen thousand dollars in cash for bail, that he might show up." Just as Branson and Williams concluded their conversation, the judge pounded his gavel to the desk. He issued an arrest warrant for Ronald Harvey, which allowed the three detectives to wrap up their futile trip to New Jersey, and head back to the nation's capital with the bad news for the prosecutors.

The next morning, Detective Branson was summoned to see John Evans, the U.S. Attorney. As he entered the office area, he spotted John Evans, who happened to be on the telephone. John Evans waved at Detective Branson to come inside. Branson took a seat, as he waited for Evans to finish his phone conversation. He figured that Evans must have been talking to another prosecutor in Philadelphia, about another murder related to the suspects. He reached this conclusion from the parts of Evan's conversation that he overheard as he entered the office. Evans listened intently, then made remarks like, "When was he killed, and do you think this one is related to the Hanafi murders?" He also asked if there were any possibility that one of the suspects in the Hanafi killings were involved. Evans finished his phone conversation, but before he could say anything Branson asked, "Who did they kill this time, and how many?" Evans told Bronson that he wasn't sure who was involved, then asked him why he was inquiring.

Evans told Branson that there was a jailhouse murder in Philadelphia on the very same day that Branson and his partners were in New Jersey for Ronald Harvey's hearing. He said the victim was a Hanafi Muslim named Sam Molten.

Sam Molten was at Holmesburg prison in Philadelphia, awaiting trial on drug charges, and apparently since he had listed himself as Muslim, the prison authorities housed him on the same cellblock as the Muslims in the Nation of Islam. Branson asked Evans how Molten was killed. Evans replied, "They stabbed him thirty-eight times." "How many guys do the officials believe are involved in this murder?" asked Branson. Evans told him that Edward Rendell, the assistant district attorney prosecuting the case, had charged four inmates so far. Then the inevitable question: Branson asked if Evans believed the two cases were related. Evans said that he believed they were related.

Evans reminded Branson that a day before the murder, on August 16th, the indictments of the eight murder suspects were published in the Philadelphia papers. The Assistant District Attorney surmised that the murder of Sam Molten was a message of solidarity to the eight suspects.

Evans had already received the information about Ronald Harvey, through the law enforcement grapevine, so he didn't even bother to ask Branson anything about their trip to New Jersey. However, Branson did ask Evans when the extradition hearing would be held for the suspects already in custody. Evans said the extradition hearing for the four in custody was set for Tuesday, August 28th. All four suspects were present in the Philadelphia court for the extradition hearing. All four fought extradition to Washington D.C. Their protest was a futile act. The judge granted the order to extradite, and the four were put on a prison bus. They were escorted by federal marshals for their arraignment in Washington, scheduled for September 4, 1973.

Detectives Branson, Jacobs, and Williams were finally relieved. Their part in the investigation had come to a successful end, netting seven indictments, four of the seven were on their way to the nation's capital, soon to be scheduled for trial.

Judge Leonard Braman, a distinguished and experienced trial judge, was given the assignment to preside over the Hanafi murder trial. At 9:00 a.m., on September 4, 1973, all four defendants; John Clark, Theodore Moody, James Price, and Jerome Sinclair stood in front of Judge Braman for their arraignment hearing. Since this was a capital murder case with seven victims, there was no consideration of bail. The arraignment was elevated to celebrity status, with the media's presence on the steps of the courthouse. Hoping to avoid the media fanfare, Judge Braman swiftly proceeded, asking the public defenders to enter a plea for the four defendants. Each defendant had his own public defender. One after the other stood with his counsel to enter a plea of not guilty. Judge Braman gave a trial date of February 6, 1974 before remanding the defendants to the custody of the federal authorities. Coincidentally, on the same day of the arraignment of the four defendants, the F.B.I. added a new fugitive to their list of the ten most wanted. Ronald Harvey now belonged to the F.B.I's elite list of ten, as well as the federal manhunt for John Griffin and William Christian. This would mean an unlimited amount of surveillance now could be employed to apprehend the fugitives.

Two Philadelphia agents with the F.B.I. were given the task to locate the fugitives through means of local surveillance. Agents Parker and Smallwood were ten-year veterans with the F.B.I., and were well versed in the many tactics of what was referred to as "street surveillance."

"Street surveillance" referred to the use of informants. The F.B.I. had many informants in the Black community at their disposal. They utilized these informants in many ways. One of the main ways to use an informant at this particular time was to infiltrate an organization. Most of the traditional civil rights organizations were known to have been thoroughly infiltrated, and the black power organizations that followed were no different in this respect.

One of the agency's informants in the Nation of Islam was a guy named Carlo Greene. Carlo was an ex-convict with a long rap sheet for burglary and rape. Carlo was also a heroin addict. The agency supported Carlo's habit with a monthly stipend, in exchange for minutes of weekly meetings at Temple #12. Carlo had an administrative position at Temple #12, which gave him access to recorded meetings.

Directly after the Hanafi killings, agents Parker and Smallwood summoned Carlo in for a meeting to find out if he were privy to any information about where the shooters were coming from. To their dismay, Carlo was in a drunk tank for three days for disorderly conduct and drug possession. When they bailed him out of jail, they ordered him to get them information on the killings, as the Washington investigators planned their sights on Philadelphia exclusively.

Carlo had reported back to the agents that there was an information blackout at Temple #12. He said, "Nobody dares to mention anything about Washington. You can't even mention the White House without people looking at you funny." About the same time, Detective Remus Williams came to Philadelphia, infiltrated Temple #12, and blew the case wide open.

Agents Parker and Smallwood were actually hoping that they wouldn't have to utilize Carlo's services to sniff out the fugitives. On September 6, 1973 the agents were given the green light to wiretap family members and known associates of the fugitives. One known associate of John Griffin and William Christian proved to be quite valuable.

Richard Dabney, a Black Muslim and ex-convict, was an associate. Dabney was one of the first wiretaps requested by the agents. For the first few weeks they didn't hear anything of value, then on September 30ᵗʰ they hit pay dirt.

Richard Danny was heard complaining on the phone to a woman about the money he owed to John 43X. Based on the list given to them by Carlo Greene, agents Parker and Smallwood were able to identify that John 43X was none other than John Griffin. Apparently, Disney owed John Griffin money from previous dealings, and Griffin had a third party call Dabney while he was on the phone complaining about giving John 43X the money, and saying that he would have to wait a few weeks because the "feds" were all over the Temple. He also said that he was not going to put his own freedom in jeopardy.

After hearing the conversation, agents Parker and Smallwood paid Dabney a visit. They informed Dabney that they had listened to his conversation regarding owing money to John 43X, and they were willing to cut a deal with him in exchange for his cooperation. Dabney stood there grinning as the agents presented him with their scenario to snag John Griffin and William Christian. Danny actually looked relieved, maybe because he didn't have the money to send John Griffin.

On October 3, 1973, F.B.I. agents in Jacksonville Florida captured John Griffin and William Christian in an apartment building. They had been hiding out in Jacksonville with their wives and children since May. Two days later, they were both extradited to Washington D.C., and arraigned for the Hanafi killings.

Ronald Harvey was the last remaining fugitive, and since his position in Philadelphia's Black Mafia was higher than the others, Harvey's resources allowed him to stay out of sight without communicating to anyone in Philadelphia, which also made for difficult surveillance on the F.B.I's behalf.

William Christian and John Griffin were given different public defenders, and now all six of the seven defendants were in custody. They would all be tried together on February 6, 1974. At the beginning of the trial, Ronald Harvey was still at-large. On the first day of trial, the prosecutors dropped a bombshell on the defense.

With the help of the prosecution, James Price's attorney motioned to have his case severed from the others, for the purpose of having Price testify as the star witness. The defense attorneys and their clients cried foul. The defense attorneys physically got into a huddle to collectively strategize their next move. They came out of the huddle a few moments later, and asked for a dismissal of charges, which Judge Braman immediately refused.

The defense argued that the prosecution hid James Price's identity as their star witness, thus violating the process of discovery. Assistant U.S. attorney Robert Shuker responded, arguing that there was no such violation because the judge who presided over the grand jury sealed the order, affecting Price's protective custody status. Shuker further argued that the seal allowed the prosecution to exclude Price from their witness list during discovery. Judge Braman agreed with the prosecution's argument and denied the defense's motion.

Anticipating that they would lose the dismissal argument, the defense team followed up with a motion to suppress James Price's testimony. Judge Braman reserved ruling on the motion immediately, but agreed to hear arguments on the issue after the prosecution had presented other portions of their case. The defendants had devastated looks on their faces. They knew the F.B.I. informants in Temple #12, and they figured that the government had received second hand information. They had no idea that James Price had confessed, and served them up to the government. The defense knew that if they weren't granted a favorable ruling on their motion to suppress, their clients wouldn't have much of a chance against the testimony of an admitted accomplice. Meanwhile, the prosecution proceeded with its case, calling the police officers who were first to arrive at the Hanafi compound on January 18, 1973.

Metropolitan police officer, Harry Hopkins testified that he and his partner were responding to a possible breaking and entering call at the Hanafi house, when they discovered the seven dead bodies, and the two wounded. Officer Hopkins described the amount of blood splatter that he and his partner observed as they found the adult victims on the bottom floor of the compound. After officer Hopkins' testimony, the prosecution called Hamaas Abdul Khaalis to testify about what he saw as he arrived home that fateful afternoon.

John Evans, and his prosecution team were worried that Khaalis' testimony would be too emotionally charged. On the morning that Khaalis was to testify, John Evans met with him in a private office in the courthouse. Evans asked Khaalis if he was sure that he could handle taking the stand. Evans told Khaalis that they only needed him on the stand to corroborate the motive for the killings. He also told Khaalis that they only needed the jury to hear him say that he had sent letters to the Black Muslim ministers, and that he believed that to be the reason his family was killed. Evans explained to Khaalis that he would go into the content of the letter himself, he didn't want Khaalis to read the letter for fear of making him appear to be antagonistic towards the Black Muslims at best, and at worst provocative.

Khaalis was reported to have a stoic look on his face in response to Evan's suggestions. Sensing his disinterest, Evans further explained to Khaalis that the reason he had explained the format of the testimony was to keep everything on course, minimizing the chance of getting into what he called "murky waters," with emotional outburst. Khaalis reported to have stood up from his chair and shouted at Evans to concern himself with the legal issues and let him (Khaalis) concern himself with his emotional stability. Evans must have had a crystal ball that fateful morning, because his biggest fear about Khaalis' testimony became a self-fulfilling prophecy.

Judge Braman entered the court, and asked the prosecution to call their next witness. John Evans called Hamaas Khaalis to the stand. His first question to Khaalis:

Q: Now, Mr. Khaalis could you tell the court your profession at the house?

A: I'm the masheer.

Q: What does the masheer mean?

A: The director, the spiritual advisor. The man defends the faith. The man who knows tricksters, murders and gangsters who deviate on Islam. As John Evans attempted to ask Hamaas Khaalis the next question, Khaalis looked over to the defense's table, and noticed that one of the defense attorneys was smiling. Khaalis became enraged, he yelled from the witness stand, "You don't have to smile, mister!" Judge Braman chimed in, "Wait a minute Mr. Khaalis, we're trying to conduct a proceeding." Khaalis looked over at the judge and said, "I don't want him smiling and smirking at me." Attempting to redirect Khaalis, Judge Braman said, "Please Mr. Khaalis just listen and respond carefully to the questions. Just look at Mr. Evans and respond carefully to the questions." Appearing defensive, Khaalis told Judge Braman that he would respond to John Evans' questions. Evans felt this was a good time to cool things off, so he asked for a bench conference and asked Mr. Khaalis to step down from the witness stand.

As Khaalis stepped down, he turned and took another look at the defense table, and almost uncontrollably, he yelled, "You killed my babies! You killed my babies, and shot my women." Once again, Judge Braman asked Mr. Khaalis to calm himself. Now directing his rage to the judge he yelled that the cutthroat niggers killed his babies, almost as if to justify his feelings of rage. Pretending not to hear Khaalis' comment, Judge Braman told him that he is in a court of law, and if he didn't get a hold of himself he would be escorted out of the courtroom and cited with contempt of court. Mr. Khaalis was reported to have stared at the judge as if his eyes had popped out of its sockets. Responding to Judge Braman, Khaalis spoke in an enraged tone, asking the judge how he would have the nerve to cite him for contempt of court when his babies were lying in a cemetery due to the actions of cutthroat gangsters. At his wits' end, Judge Braman told Khaalis that he had heard enough, and asked the marshals to escort Mr. Khaalis out of the courtroom. Then the judge turned to instruct the jury on Khaalis' outburst.

Judge Braman told the jury to keep their minds open, and to that end, no one should discuss either between themselves or with others the events that recently occurred. To make sure that got the crux of his message, he reiterated, "And I mean literally that you are not to discuss this." Unsatisfied with the judge's instructions to the jury, the defense team motioned for a mistrial due to Khaalis' prejudicial, emotional outburst. Judge Braman excused the jury to hear the defense's argument for a mistrial.

The judge listened intently to the defense argument. Durward Taylor, part of John Griffin and William Christian's defense counsel, argued that the judge may have faith in the jury, but he didn't believe that a jury only eight days old would be able to exclude Khaalis' outburst from their memory, when deciding the guilt or innocence of his clients.

After hearing the argument, Judge Braman turned the tables on Mr. Taylor, saying that time was the main reason that he has faith in this jury. Judge Braman told the defense that the eight day old jury works in their favor. He added that the jury has enough time to weigh other evidence, thus giving less weight to an emotional outburst from a family member of the victims. Then he denied their motion. Judge Braman then turned to John Evans, admonishing him for Khaalis' behavior in court. He told Evans, "Mr. Khaalis is through testifying in my court, so if you haven't finished with him, consider him finished." John Evans just looked at the judge and nodded his head in compliance, just as Khaalis had done to him before his testimony.

Attempting to strike while the iron was hot, Durward Taylor asked for an immediate ruling on the suppression of James Price's testimony. The Judge smiled, after realizing that the defense was trying to come away with some type of victory after the day's trial and errors. Judge Braman told counsel that he really doesn't like to be rushed into rendering a decision, then he smiled again and decided to allow the defense to save a little of its face. He looked down at his calendar, and gave March 27th for his date of decision.

The date of the judge's ruling on James Price's testimony became common knowledge, because only two days before the ruling, a radio broadcast aired a message from the Nation of Islam that seemed to be directly related to the trial in Washington. The message came from Louis Farrakhan, the leader of Temple #7 in Harlem. Temple #7 was Malcolm X's temple, before he was assassinated.

In his message, minister Louis Farrakhan said, "Let this be a warning to the enemies of Muhammad. Let this be a warning to those of you who would allow yourselves to be used as an instrument of a wicked government against our rise. Be careful because when the government is tired of you, they're going to dump you back in the laps of our people, and though Elijah Muhammad is a merciful man, and will say, come in, and forgive you. Yet the ranks of black people today, there are younger men and women rising up, who have no forgiveness in them for traitors and stool pigeons, and they will execute you, as soon as your identity is known."

After James Price from his jail cell heard the minister's speech, that some considered to be a veiled threat, the suppression of the testimony would become a moot point. James Price had made a decision to change his plans, but the Nation of Islam would have some plans of its own, for the star witness for the prosecution.

CHAPTER NINE
Witness for the Prosecution

On March 26, 1974, the day before he was to rule on the suppression of James Price's testimony, Judge Braman received a note from Price's attorney. The note was marked urgent. As Judge Braman sat in his chambers, he thought about one of Murphy's laws; whatever can happen, will happen. He likened the note to Pandora's Box.

After reading the note, Judge Braman thought to himself that the prosecution may never recover from this. Then he wrote seven words on a notepad, as a reminder for tomorrow's hearing; Price to face possible charges of contempt.

Court reconvened the following morning, at nine o'clock. Two of the defense seemed to be in voracious moods, smiling like Cheshire cats. They were either very confident that Judge Braman was prepared to rule in their favor, or they were given the same information the judge received just a day earlier.

As Judge Braman raised his gavel to bring the court to session, he took a visual picture of the participants. One face was unrecognizable, as a regular in the courtroom. A black man with a shaved baldhead, wearing a black suit and a bright red bow-tie, sat behind the defense's table. As the judge brought the court to session, the smiling defense attorneys were on their feet, asking for a ruling on the suppression. Judge Braman cleared his throat, and stated that an issue had come to his attention that demanded the court's immediate priority. He then asked that both the prosecution and defense teams approach the bench. As the attorneys gathered around to hear about his urgent matter, Judge Braman picked up the note, and handed it to William Shannon, one of James Price's attorneys.

The judge then asked Mr. Shannon to read the note to the other attorneys gathered at the bench. Mr. Shannon shook his head in agreement and began to read. "Dear Judge Braman, we have just been notified by our client, James Price, that he has decided not to testify for the government, and that he has hired another attorney to represent him in this case, as he would like to remove Mr. Farqhar and myself as his counsel. Respectfully, William T. Shannon."

John Evans and Robert Shuker were livid, and the defense was still smiling. John Evans asked Judge Braman to allow him to put James Price on the stand immediately, to account for his change of heart. Judge Braman responded, "Counselor, that's exactly what I'm going to do." The judge recessed the jury, and cleared the courtroom of spectators and reporters. Everyone left in the courtroom were connected to the case, as attorney, defendant, and witness, with one notable exception: the unrecognizable bald man who sat behind the defense.

Before proceeding with James Price on the stand, the judge asked the bald man to state his business. Speaking in a baritone voice, the bald man said, "I am Donald Plesante, and I am here to represent my client." The judge told Mr. Pleasante that he was familiar with almost every defense attorney within the District of Columbia, but failed to recognize his name. He then asked Mr. Plesante if he were licensed to practice law in D.C. Donald Plesante answered in the affirmative. Then the judge paused and looked at the defense team, who didn't seem surprised about any of this. Then he glanced over at the prosecution, who looked as if they were awakening from a long sleep. Already knowing the answer, Judge Braman asked Donald Plesante to name his client. Pleasante said, "James Price is my client your honor." Now smiling himself, the Judge told Mr. Plesante that he didn't know where he went to law school, but Washington courts didn't allow defendants to change attorneys, absent legal procedure. He reminded Mr. Plesante that they were not conducting a preliminary hearing, but were in the middle of a capital murder trial.

Perhaps feeling the need to redeem himself, Mr. Plesante responded to the judge's query of his jurisprudence. He informed Judge Braman that he was well versed in criminal law procedure, and reminded the judge that James Price was not yet on trial, since his case was severed from the others. He argued that the severance of his case should allow Price to change attorneys without upsetting the trial of his alleged co-defendants. Judge Braman told Mr. Plesante that he was correct on one account, that Price's case was severed due to his choosing to cooperate with the authorities, thus becoming a witness for the prosecution. He said, "However, that may all change this morning." Then Judge Braman instructed Mr. Plesante to leave the courtroom so that those involved in the case could discuss James Price's status. James Price was called to the witness stand.

James Price seemed a little nervous, as he walked to the stand in his oversized suit, much too large for his five and a half foot stature. The judge asked Price flatly whether he intended to testify for the government or not. Arrogantly, Price said "Not." The Judge then warned Price to rethink his decision because he could face additional criminal and civil charges of contempt of court. Judge Braman warned Price that this was a very serious matter, because Price's case had been severed to accommodate his testimony, as a witness for the prosecution. James looked up at the judge as if he were looking at someone who was saying something insanely to him. He told the judge that in refusing to testify, he was subjecting himself to the same charges as his co-defendants. To twenty-three counts, that included murder, robbery and conspiracy. Again in an arrogant tone, Price said forgive me if I don't get upset about a contempt of court charge. Then he said, "I simply do not wish to cooperate with the government in this matter." The Judge had a look on his face that said he had heard enough, then he asked James Price to step down from the witness chair.

After the bailiff called the jury back, Donald Plesante also returned to the courtroom, and asked to be heard on the petition to replace Price's current counsel. Already displeased with the Price matter altogether, the Judge decided to listen to Mr. Plesante's argument, but he told Mr. Plesante that he would need some background information on him before hearing his argument. Judge Braman surprised Mr. Plesante with his first question, asking him to state his religious affiliation. Appearing to be annoyed, Mr. Plesante asked Jude Braman to explain the relevance of his religious affiliation, in giving Price effective counsel. Judge Braman asked Mr. Plesante to stop dancing around his questions and answer it, or to stop wasting the court's time. Realizing that he had no choice, if he wanted to represent James Price, Mr. Plesante said, I am a Muslim your honor. Judge Braman then asked Mr. Plesante if he were counsel for other members in the Nation of Islam. Still annoyed by the line of questions, Mr. Plesante reluctantly said yes. The judge then told Donald Plesante that he could give him the decision immediately, an unequivocal no! Explaining the rationale for his decision, the judge said that since the people implicated in the case by Mr. Price are also members of the Nation of Islam, there are clear conflicts of interest issues. Some of the investigators in the courtroom were wondering who sent Mr. Plesante to Washington, all the way from the state of Ohio to represent Mr. Price, just as he decided not to testify for the officials from the Nation of Islam.

One of the initial investigators, Detective Jacobs, decided not to visit court that morning. Instead, the detective sat at his desk reading a newspaper article about the trial. The article eluded to the anticipated testimony of the prosecution's star witness. As he read the news article, Detective Jacobs debated whether he should have gone to court that morning, to hear testimony. As he debated his decision, the phone rang. He answered the phone with his "stock and trade" greeting, "Jacobs here." Detective Remus walked into Jacob's office just as he reached to answer the phone. Remus wondered why Jacobs was smiling with his ear to the phone, although he said nothing but his name, he thanked whomever he was talking to as he hung up the phone. Williams asked, "What happened, did you win the Irish sweepstakes?" Jacobs replied, "No, but we won the Black Muslim sweep." Jacobs just stood there smiling in front of Williams, waiting to see if Williams could guess what he knew. Then, finally he said, "I thought you were quick. That was one of Chicago's finest. They just arrested Ronald Harvey."

Ronald Harvey was the last fugitive on the F.B.I's ten most wanted list to be captured. Harvey was indicted with the others in August, but had skipped bail in the murders of Major Coxson, and his step-daughter Lita. He was extradited from Chicago to Washington a few days later. Since the trial was in its sixth week, Harvey was guaranteed to be tried alone.

The next morning of the trial, John Evans informed Judge Braman that Ronald Harvey was in the custody of the metropolitan police and that his arraignment was forthcoming. After John Evans informed the judge of Harvey's status, the judge asked the prosecution to call its next witness.

James Price and Amina Khaalis were the last witnesses the government expected to testify before the government rested its case. Since James Price balked at testifying, the prosecution only had Ms. Khaalis' testimony left before resting. Amina Khaalis, the sole competent witness in the Hanafi massacre, took the stand. Ms. Khaalis walked gracefully to the stand, as John Evans, in a soft voice, asked her to describe the events on January 18, 1973.

Ms. Khaalis looked at the defendants, as she took a few moments to compose herself before speaking. Then she started with describing the beginning of the day as a normal day. She said that she was downstairs with her three year old baby brother Abdullah, and her daughter Khadyja. She said her father's second wife Bibi was upstairs with three of the other babies in the house, and her older brother was on the third floor eating his lunch. She said a little after two o'clock there was a knock on the door, and since Muslim women were not permitted to open doors for men, she called her brother Daud down from the third floor. She stayed in the kitchen with the children while Daud went to see who was at the door. She heard two distinct voices in a conversation with her brother about Islam, so he opened the door. Then she heard Daud greet the men, then leave them at the door to get the book. Daud returned with the book, then left once more to retrieve change for the two. When he returned the last time, Ms. Khaalis said it sounded as if another person had joined the two men at the door, but the third man was asking about doing some work for them. A few minutes later, she heard this loud commotion at the door, then the three men were inside the house, waving guns, and telling them to lie down on the floor. According to Ms. Khaalis, this is when one of the men snatched her daughter from her arms, and yanked little Abdullah out of his high chair. She testified that it was the last time that she saw her daughter and little brother alive. Ms. Khaalis stated that after they were asked to get on the floor, they were then forced down to the basement, and a few minutes later Bibi was also brought to the basement. They were all instructed to lie down on the floor and clothes were placed over all of their heads. About ten minutes later, one of the men brought Abdul down to the basement as well. Abdul had gone shopping with Abdul Hamaas Khaalis (the masher) and his first wife, so Amina had assumed that the men had all of the occupants of the house, but Abdul had returned alone. Minutes after they told Abdul to join the others on the basement floor, they began to fire their weapons at those on the basement floor. Amina states that at this point she began to lose consciousness. When Amina Khaalis finished describing the massacre, the entire courtroom was silent, and remained that way for about two minutes. Then John Evans asked her if she could identify any of the men in the courtroom who were at her house on the day of the massacre. She pointed at two of the four defendants on trial. After Ms. Khaalis' testimony, the prosecution rested its case.

The first two weeks of the defense case was filled with acquaintances, siblings, and spouses of the defendants. They were all there as character witnesses, and some even as alibi witnesses. They spoke of how the defendants, all of whom were fathers, loved children and would never do anything to harm anyone's children.

An acquaintance of John Clarke, a fellow member of the Nation of Islam, testified that John Clark was at Temple #12 all day, and hadn't left for home until about ten o'clock that evening. James Griffin testified on his brother's behalf making similar proclamations of having seen John Griffin around the apartment on that fateful day. The prosecutor cross-examined some of the character/alibi witnesses, using physical evidence found in Washington. John Evans asked several of the witnesses. "Well, if he was at home with you, how do you suppose his fingerprints were found in a downtown motel in Washing, D.C?" Evans also asked, "Well, if he was at home, who was it that made a collect call to your house, from a payphone in Washington, on the day of the murders?" After the two weeks of character/alibi witness testimony, the defense sought to recall witnesses for the prosecution.

They cross-examined Sarah Robinson, the chambermaid at the downtown motel, who identified William Christian. Although she appeared to be quite nervous, Ms. Robinson didn't waiver from her earlier testimony. She identified William Christian a second time in the court, as one of eight men she saw at the motel on the day of the murders. The defense would cross-examine Amina Khaalis next.

Ms. Khaalis was as poised and confident in the cross-examination, as she was in direct testimony. The defense attempted to poke a hole in her identification to the defendants. For three days, they grilled Ms. Khaalis about her initial identification of the defendants.

At the line-up on May 3, 1973, Ms. Khaalis had only identified one suspect, James Price. The other two, Theodore Moody and John Clark, she said, "They strongly resembled the men that were at our house." That wasn't considered a positive identification. Again she identified James Price's picture in court, but identified John Griffin as the man who snatched her daughter from her arms.

The defense scored a few points with the jury, when they asked her to define "strongly resembled," by showing her honesty, Ms. Khaalis admitted that since she was lying on the floor when most of the men were in the room with her, she didn't get a full view of their faces. She said she could only positively identify two of the defendants. After the defense's cross, they too rested their case.

Immediately after the defense team finished, the attorney representing Jerome Sinclair, the fifth defendant, with whom the prosecutors admitted to having no physical evidence or witnesses connecting him with the others, asked for a dismissal of charges against his client. Counsel for Sinclair argued that the government failed to meet its burden of proof against their client, and motioned for a dismissal on all charges connected with the case. The only testimony that linked Jerome Sinclair to the Hanafi murders was James Price's grand jury testimony, which couldn't be verified since Price balked at testifying in open court. Judge Braman agreed, and dismissed all charges against Jerome Sinclair. Sinclair was extradited back to Philadelphia, to stand trial for the $52,000 robbery of the Yellow Cab Company.

Both the prosecution, and the defense took a full day to present their closing arguments, before sending the jury to deliberate. The jury deliberated for thirteen hours before returning with guilty verdicts on all counts, for the four remaining defendants. The convictions carried mandatory life sentences, but the actual sentencing would be rendered a month later. According to a journalist, the four defendants displayed no emotion when the foreman of the jury read the verdict.

The entire trial lasted thirteen weeks, with the prosecution calling one hundred and thirty-five witnesses, with over five hundred exhibits entered as evidence. The cost of the trial totaled over fifty thousand dollars, which was the most expensive, non-political trial in the nation's capital in 1974.

Although the trial was long and expensive, and netted four convictions, the prosecution was far from being finished. They had two other defendants, James Price and Ronald Harvey, yet to prosecute, and they were still conducting an investigation into who gave the order to murder the Hanafis.

A day after the conviction of his four co-defendants were announced, Ronald Harvey was rushed to D.C. General Hospital, suffering from cardiac arrest. Ronald Harvey had suffered a heart attack, and was in crucial condition. Harvey stayed in the hospital for a month before being sent back to the D.C. jail. The day after his return to prison, his four convicted co-defendants were sentenced to twenty years to life for each murder which totaled one hundred and forty years for each defendant.

Ronald Harvey's trial began October 1974. John Evans led the prosecution team in Harvey's trial. Evans identified Harvey as "Mr. Enforcer," because based on the testimony from the detective Remus Williams, James Price had described Harvey as the leader, who gave the order to kill the five babies, and adults at the house. Harvey's trial lasted four and a half weeks. On November 20, 1974, the jury returned a guilty verdict to Ronald Harvey.

After Harvey's trial, U.S. Assistant Attorney Robert Shuker said, "The Hanafi massacre was one of the most atrocious crimes that any judicial system has had to deal with." Judge Braman set Harvey's sentencing date for the first week in 1975. Upon sentencing, Ronald Harvey would be sent to New Jersey, to stand trial for the murders of Major Coxson and his stepdaughter. This left one defendant for prosecution--James Price.

James Price was sent back to Philadelphia to stand trial for the murder of Myer Abrams, the junk dealer, robbed and killed by Price a few months after the Hanafi killings. Price was scheduled to go on trial for the Hanafi murders on January 7, 1975. He was also subpoenaed to appear in front of another grand jury, to answer questions about the person(s) responsible for giving the order to murder the Hanafis. Ironically, James Price was sent to Holmesburg prison to await trial, the same prison that housed his co-defendants in the Hanafi trial. An event at Holmesburg would turn irony into a profound error for the prison officials, as well as for the city of Philadelphia.

CHAPTER TEN

A Hanging at Holmesburg

On November 20, 1974, U.S. Assistant Attorneys John Evans and Robert Shuker were in a celebratory mood. They had just successfully prosecuted five of the seven defendants in the Hanafi murders. James Price was the last defendant in the case, yet to be prosecuted. Both Mr. Evans and Mr. Shakur thought that Price would spare them another long trial. They had counted on Price to be their star witness in both trials against his co-defendants, but at the last minute Price balked at testifying. Evans and Shuker's error in judgment about Price's willingness to testify cost them to lose one defendant, Jerome Sinclair.

The government's case against Sinclair was very weak, and so they were relying on Price to connect the dots, as to who did what to the Hanafis. Evans and Shuker now had about forty-five days to prepare, before James Price was to go on trial. Simultaneously, they were also preparing to bring Price back to the grand jury, with the hope of getting him to name the leader(s) who gave the order to kill the Hanafis. They were willing to let Price plead to lesser counts in exchange for his cooperation in naming those responsible for the massacre.

Price was sent back to Philadelphia to await trial for the robbery and murder that he racked up during his crime spree. Price was sent to Holmesburg prison. Located in the northeast section of Philadelphia, Holmesburg was a waiting station for prisoners who were held over for trial, or sentencing in a case, before going up state. Holmesburg officials had witnessed many violent confrontations among inmates.

Sam Molten, the Hanafi Muslim who was murdered by Black Muslim prisoners, was murdered at Holmesburg prison. There were many murders in Holmesburg during the notorious street gang period as well, but the most controversial murder at Holmesburg, in which prison officials would be forced from their jobs, and municipal judges would assert a conspiracy, was yet to come.

The Muslim population at Holmesburg was housed on "D" block. Prior to the murder of Sam Molten, inmates were asked their religious affiliation, and if they were Muslim, they would be housed on "D" block. The prison officials were either unconcerned, or ignorant to the fact that Islam had many denominations or sects, as does Christianity. After the headlines of the Hanafi murder indictments in Philadelphia, and the subsequent murder of Sam Molten, prison officials started housing Hanafi Muslims separate from Muslims in the Nation of Islam.

"D" block was not only used to house the Nation of Islam Muslim population, it was also used as an isolation block for inmates with infractions from other blocks.

On December 29, 1974, at about eight in the morning, Calvin Hunter, a new inmate housed in "C" block, was sent to "D" block for isolation. According to prison records, and Calvin Hunter's statement to the police, he was being isolated because he had gotten into an argument with one of the guards on "C" block. When sent to "D" block for punishment, he was locked into cell #453. Calvin Hunter decided to make the best of his stay, so he pulled out a cowboy book that another inmate had loaned him, and began to read.

According to Calvin's statement, he was reading for about an hour, then decided to take a nap for an hour before lunch. Calvin said he had slept about forty-five minutes, before he was awakened by the screams of another inmate, a few cells a way.

Calvin awakened to hear someone screaming, "Don't kill me, help!" Calvin said he heard the man repeat his cry for help three times. Then, according to Calvin, the same voice yelled, "They're trying to kill me," about four times. Calvin said he didn't know if someone was just messing around, or if the person was seriously in danger. He said he immediately went to his cell door, and looked outside but couldn't see anyone. He said then he looked down the block, and could tell that the screams were coming from the end of the cellblock, about four cells away from where he was housed. A few minutes later there was a silence, and Calvin said he continued to look outside to see who was on the block.

About ten minutes into the silence, Calvin said he noticed three men coming from the direction of the screams. One of the men, who is described as tall and dark skinned, is familiar to Calvin. He didn't remember the man's name, but said he knew him from the neighborhood. The other two, a dark skinned, stocky man, with the letters "LT" on his pants, and a younger, short, light skinned man were both unfamiliar to Calvin.

Calvin said he yelled out to the familiar man, asking him "What's happening?" According to Calvin, the tall dark skinned man looked in his direction, and said, "Nothing that concerns you." The other two men continued walking past Calvin's cell, but the tall dark skinned man stopped, and asked Calvin why he was there on "D" block. Calvin had told him that he had gotten into an argument with a guard on "C" block. After Calvin answered his question, the tall, dark skinned man joined his associates and walked off the block.

About thirty minutes later, a guard brought a lunch tray to Calvin and informed him that he could go to the television room to watch the football game if he behaved himself. Calvin promised the guard that he would behave himself, and went off to watch the game. He said he sat in the television room for close to twenty minutes, when the tall dark skinned man who he had spoken to on the block came in and asked him if he wanted to attend their Muslim meeting. Calvin told him that he didn't wish to attend, and the tall dark skinned man asked him why. He told the man that he just didn't feel like it. After the tall, dark skinned man left him alone, he went back to watching the game, but from where he was seated, he could see the Muslims getting ready to start their meeting.

They were going from cell to cell, asking everyone if they were coming to the meeting. Calvin noticed that none of the Muslims went past his cell, towards the end of the cell bock to ask if anyone was attending the meeting. The meeting was held in a cell towards the front of the cellblock, near where Calvin was watching the game.

Calvin said he noticed that there were two guys standing directly outside of the cell, guarding and meeting. Calvin also noticed when the meeting was over, and the Muslims started filing out of the cell about fifteen minutes later. He thought to himself that the Muslim's meeting was unusually short. He even heard one of the guards comment about how short the Muslim's meeting was that day.

As he watched them leave the meeting, he noticed that some of them came directly into the television room, and sat right behind him. The tall, dark skinned man returned to the television room with the younger light skinned man that he had walked with earlier on the cellblock. The young light skinned man sat right beside Calvin, as the tall, dark skinned man stood behind them. According to Calvin, the tall, dark skinned man told him that he should have attended the meeting. Calvin said he turned around and just said, "Oh yeah." The football game was at half-time, he sat down again to watch the game. At this point, the guards were changing shifts.

They began to check the cells on the block, and Calvin thought to himself that they were going to lock him back in his cell so that he could finish his isolation for the earlier argument with the guard. He noticed the guard was checking off names on the pad, as he walked passed each cell. When the guard reached the cell four doors down from Calvin's cell, he went inside. The guard came out a few minutes later and locked the cell. Then he walked back to the front of the cellblock, and spoke with another guard. After they spoke for about two minutes, the two guards walked back down to the cell that one guard had locked. When they reached the cell, one of the guards yelled, "Go on down," that was a code for the inmates to get in their cells for a lockup.

Calvin watched the inmates. As everyone walked back to their cells, no one looked surprised. He felt that something was wrong, because it wasn't lockup time, no one had said anything. He continued to look out his cell door. Then he noticed the lieutenant, and some other guards coming down block, past his cell.

One of the guards yelled for someone to bring him a chair. A few more guards came running past Calvin's cell, and he yelled to them. No one stopped, so he yelled again, "Hey!" A guard stopped, and asked him what he wanted. Calvin asked the guard if the guy was dead, and the guard asked Calvin what he knew. Calvin told the guard that he heard a guy yelling from that direction before lunch. The guard asked Calvin what the guy was yelling, and Calvin told him the guy yelled two things, "Don't kill me, help!" and "They're trying to kill me." The guard immediately removed Calvin from "D" block, and took him into the warden's office.

Calvin waited in the warden's office for two hours before anyone came in to speak with him. He expected to speak with the warden, but two plain clothes detectives were there instead. Detective Roosevelt Hall, and Detective James McCauley were from homicide, and were anxious to hear Calvin's story.

Detective Hall asked Calvin to tell them what he had heard, and what he saw. When Calvin finished telling the detectives about the morning's events, Detective Hall passed him a stack of pictures. The pictures were of inmates, currently at Holmesburg. The first picture the detective showed Calvin was the picture of the victim. Detective Hall asked Calvin if he knew the man. Calvin said that he had seen the man before, but he didn't know his name. Detective Hall said his name was James "Bubbles" Price. Calvin's eyes did a double take. Repeating what the Detective said, he said, "This is James Price." Detective McCauley asked Calvin why he was so shocked after hearing the victim's name. Calvin laughed and asked the Detectives if they knew about Price's case. "You seem to know something about him, why don't you tell us what you know about his case," replied Detective Hall. Calvin said James Price was the stool pigeon in the Hanafi case in Washington. He added that he heard that Price was responsible for the Muslims at Temple #12 getting convicted. Then raising his voice Calvin said, "It all makes sense now." Detective McCauley asked him what about it made sense. Calvin paused to consider what he was divulging to the police, then he just blurted it out.

He told them that one of the guys he saw walking from the direction of the noise he recognized from his neighborhood, and had heard that this person he recognized was convicted in the Hanafi murders. Detectives Hall and McCauley looked at each other, and Hall said, "It sounds like a breakdown in security, some heads are going to roll for this." As the detectives continued to question Calvin Hunter, one of the guards from the morning shift on "D" block, sat in his car, contemplating his future.

The guard was terrified by the whole event, and he thought to himself that this jailhouse murder would bring some bad consequences, not only to himself but to the others indirectly involved as well. The murder of James Price on December 29, 1974 would become one of the most controversial jailhouse murders in Philadelphia's history. Not only was Price placed in the same prison with those he was thought to have incriminated in the Hanafi massacre, during his grand jury testimony, but he was placed on the same cell block with three of them, and in the same cell with one of his co-defendants. In the months to follow, guards would lose their jobs, the federal prosecutors would lose the opportunity to discover who gave the order to murder the Khaalis family, and a family would be made to participate at the expense of their identities and possibly their lives.

CHAPTER ELEVEN

Deny Thy Father, Deny Thy Name

As my two sisters and I ran all around our usually tidy house on Sunday afternoon, there was a frantic knock on the door. The knock distracted us from our game of tag. Mother was in the kitchen preparing dinner, and closer to the door, so none of us bothered to come downstairs and see who was knocking. The date was December 29, 1974. Only four days after Christmas. This meant that my sisters and I had only three days left on our holiday vacation before returning to school.

After we heard mother respond to the knock, we returned to our play. However, after we heard the frantic knocker's voice, my older sister Dana, who was ten years old, made us stop playing. Dana and my other sister Darshell wanted to eavesdrop on my mother's conversation. I was only seven, and was outnumbered by the females in the house, so I had to give in to their request.

We all listened intently to my mother's conversation on the lower floor. The first thing I heard my mother say was 'What's wrong, Silas?" Silas was a childhood friend of my mother. He would come over every few months, and play a game of cards with my mother, step-father and my aunt. He was always in his work uniform when he came over to the house. In my youth, I thought Mr. Silas was a police officer, because his uniform resembled a policeman's uniform. On that day, I came to know the true nature of M. Silas' employment.

There seemed to be a long pause in conversation between my mother's question of "what's wrong," and Mr. Silas' response. When he finally spoke, he said, "Everything's wrong Jeanette. James Price was found hanging in his cell today." There was another long pause, but this time it was from my mother. "What!" she exclaimed. He repeated himself using Price's nickname. "Bubbles was found hanging in his cell today." What happened, Silas?" mother asked. Silas said, "Jeanette, all I can tell you is that I am afraid for my life, and my livelihood. I was guarding the "D" block when it happened." I heard mother let out a sound of annoyance, then she said, "You still haven't told me what happened." Silas said, "I'll tell you, but I'm just so scared. Then he told the tale.

He said, "I came on shift at eight o'clock this morning, and as usual, I was assigned to guard "D" block. When I came on duty, the guys were up in front of their cell doors, and we conducted our usual head count. At about eleven o'clock this morning, the guys from the block were taken outside for exercise. Then after lunch they were brought back inside. Everything seemed to be normal, except for the Muslim meeting after lunch, which was unusually short. The entire block is practically made up of Muslims, so their meetings tended to run past my shift. Anyway, after they met for about fifteen minutes, I started to do my rounds, checking each cell, as I prepared to end my shift. I checked each cell on the block. As I reached cell #457, I noticed legs swinging from side to side. I thought someone was doing exercise in the cell, then I looked closer, and saw James Price swinging by a rope tied around the light fixture in the cell."

Mother suddenly became curious as to where Silas' confession was leading. She asked him bluntly, "Silas, why you telling me all of this?" Responding quickly, Silas said, "Jeanette, I'm telling you because the rumor on the block is that there is a prisoner who was placed on the block for disciplinary reasons. Anyway he supposedly witnessed Price walking toward his cell with three guys a few hours earlier. I don't know if he is telling the truth or not, but this was the last time Price was seen alive." Mother said, "Well, aren't you gonna tell me what you came to tell me, Silas? Who was walking with Price? Silas said, "The guy claims that one of the three walking with Price was Ducky."

After that, my sisters and I heard another long pause, but frankly we didn't need to hear anymore. Silas did not only know mother from childhood, but he also knew my father as well. My sisters and I were only too familiar with the nickname "Ducky;" it was our father's nickname. Mother always used it when speaking about father, or speaking to him on the telephone. Our paternal grandmother also used it when she spoke to him or lovingly about him, but called him by the first two initials of his name, J.W., when she was angry with him.

At seven, I couldn't fully digest everything that Mr. Silas had discussed with mother that afternoon, but my seven year old intuition told me that my father was in trouble, once again. Before Mr. Silas' visit, we barely heard father's name, nickname, initials or otherwise, mentioned in our house for quite a long time.

Mother had remarried in December of 1973, about six months after the last time any of us had seen father in person. My sisters and I were shown a picture of our father in August of 1973, with the caption, "wanted fugitive." Mother had scolded the neighbor responsible for showing us the picture. Everyone in our neighborhood knew our last names, and had seen our father pick us up for weekend visits. So we weren't hiding anything from anyone, but mother didn't want us hurt from the headlines.

After Mr. Silas left our house, mother came upstairs to see what her threesome was getting into. She had a suspicious look on her pretty brown face, as if she were trying to figure out whether we had heard any of her conversation. Although she was suspicious, mother never asked us if we heard anything at all. In fact, Mr. Silas never returned after that last visit, and months would pass before any of us heard anything else concerning father.

I recall a visit to my aunt's house about nine months after the incident that December. I was playing stickball in my aunt's backyard, when she called me in for dinner. My aunt was a television addict. She had a television in every room, except the bathroom. She had a little thirteen inch, black and white television that she kept atop the kitchen counter, so that she could watch the news while she cooked. When I came in for dinner that day, the news had just started. I heard the reporter say that they just rendered a verdict in the James Price murder trial, convicting

John Griffin on all counts of murder in the first degree. When I heard my name, I immediately looked up to the television to see the person's face; of course it was my father's face. My aunt must have thought about what my mother would say if she knew I had heard the broadcast, so she quickly turned off the television, but I pretended as if I hadn't heard the report.

When I returned home, I acted as if everything was normal. I didn't mention the news report to anyone, but I understood the implications of what I had heard. To me, this meant that my sisters and I would probably never see my father again. It had already been two years since we had any contact with our father. Although mother had remarried, and we had a step-father, who treated us like his own, I still missed my father. When I went to bed that night in August, I cried myself to sleep, and made myself a promise not to forget my father, but as time elapsed, I didn't miss him as much. I didn't know it then, but my father's trial and subsequent conviction of James Price's murder would be very ironic, because weeks before Price's murder, father appealed his conviction in the Hanafi murders and was awaiting a decision from the federal courts. Then nearly three weeks after he was charged in Price's murder he won his appeal for a new trial. With Price's testimony being the only link the prosecutor's had to tie father with the crime, one could imagine that the federal prosecutors would have their work cut out for them in retrying father for the Hanafi murders. We didn't have a clue then, but the prosecutors would pull out every trick imaginable to secure a second conviction against my father. We also didn't know that our lives were about to change in a way that we could have never imagined.

In January of 1976, five months before my ninth birthday, I joined the cub scouts, and was impatiently waiting for spring to join the Little League team at school. I still loved my father, but thinking about his situation became more of an inconvenience to my sisters' and me, as we desired to live as normal children.

I will never forget February 8, 1976 for as long as I shall live. You might say it was my family's version of Pearl Harbor. Prior to February 8th, we were trying as hard as we could to live a normal life in the projects of Abbottsford homes in Philadelphia. I can vividly recall the knock on the door at five thirty that evening. It was already dark outside, and quite cold.

Mother who had just come home from work, opened the door. There stood two tall white men, with close crop military style haircuts, and black trench coats. They flashed their badges, and announced that they were with the F.B.I. Mother seemed quite shaken by their announcement. She put her hand over her mouth, as if to be preparing to throw up her lunch. Then she motioned to the agents to sit down. Finally, one of the agents, whom I perceived to be the senior person in charge, began to state their reason for visiting us on that cold night in February.

He said, "Mrs. Griffin, we have reasons to believe that you were privy to a conversation in which your husband discussed information about the Hanafi murders in Washington, three years ago. Mother corrected the agent, she said "First of all, my name is no longer Griffin, it's Mrs. Bertha, and my husband isn't home from work yet. As for John Griffin, we've been divorced for six years now, and I didn't know about his whereabouts then, and I don't care about where he is now." The agent apologized to my mother for calling her Mrs. Griffin, and then he dropped the mother of all bombs on us.

He told mother that the F.B.I had an authorized wiretap on anyone associated with father in 1973, which meant our phone was tapped. He continued, saying that they had recorded a conversation in 1973, in which mother asked father about the weapons used in the Hanafi killings. Apparently mother had read a newspaper article stating that investigators had linked the weapons in the case to Philadelphia. The agent said that my father had incriminated himself in that conversation, and they needed mother to come to Washington, and testify about the contents of that conversation. Mother didn't believe that they had taped the conversation, so she asked, "If you have a tape of a conversation, why do you need me?" The agents informed my mother that without her confirmation of the contents of the conversation in front of a jury, the tape would be no good. Mother's hands began to shake, as the agent continued his pitch to get her to testify. When he finished his pitch, mother had summoned enough strength to hold her hand steady while telling the agent what she thought of his proposition.

She spoke almost in a whisper, it was the first time I had seen my mother lose her voice. She said, "I don't remember the conversation, so I cannot corroborate or confirm something I do not remember." The agent replied, saying that they didn't expect mother to remember the conversation that occurred three years ago. He told her that they would play the tape, with the hope of jogging her memory. The agents had already made us feel as if we were in Hiroshima with the first news they dropped on us, next was Nagasaki.

He told mother, with us standing two feet away, that our lives were in danger. He said, since they had anticipated subpoenaing her to testify for father's re-trial in Washington, they added her name to the list of witnesses for the prosecution during the discovery portion of pre-trial motions. Mother failed to see the significance of that bit of information until he added that father, and his co-defendants had access to the list. Hesitantly, the agent added that they had "street sources" that informed them about a potential contract that was taken out on three people on the prosecution's witness list. He said, "You were one of the three, and knowing how these guys kill, that means your entire family is in danger."

Mother shouted at the agent, "John would never harm me or his children. This is a lie!" The agent replied, "It's the man who gave John and the others the order to kill that you have to worry about. The leadership of your ex-husband's organization is worried. They don't know who said what to their loved ones about the murders. Your ex-husband is already considered a possible weak link because of the James Price murder conviction. They are not going to take any chance with you as a witness against him; they don't know what he told you, and that's what frightens them."

Mother was very angry at this point, and a tear streamed down her face. She said, "You are giving us a death sentence, and my children and I had nothing to do with any of this. Who gave you the right to put me on your witness list, without asking me before you did it. If anything happens to my children, or myself, our blood will be on your hands. I have nothing but contempt for what you've done to us."

The agent then told mother that the only way out of this mess was for all of us to leave Philadelphia forever, and allow them to put us in their witness protection program. He explained what going into the program would mean for us. It meant we may never be able to return to our home, we couldn't have any contact with family or friends, and we would be given a new identity.

The agent eventually won mother with his scare tactic. He told mother about another family they had offered witness protection to, but the family declined because they didn't want severed family ties. The agent said the whole family was found murdered two days after their refusal to participate.

That evening of February 8ᵗ, our clothes were packed, we were escorted by U.S. Marshals, and we left Abbottsford Homes forever. We stayed at the Benjamin Franklin hotel, in Center City Philadelphia, before heading out of state. I guess Benjamin Franklin served as our "safe house."
It was a totally foreign experience for all of us. We stayed in the beautiful hotel, with room service at our beck and call, yet we couldn't enjoy it because of all of the uncertainty. My sisters and I didn't realize at the time that we would never return to see any of our friends, or teachers. We simply did not understand the permanence of the whole thing. We had lost our father, and we knew where he was, so it wasn't quite the same as a death, but to not return to the people and places that defined who we were was similar to death for us. I don't think it really hit us until we arrived in Virginia.

We arrived in Richmond, Virginia about a week after we were put into protective custody, and we had no idea that we would literally be starting our lives over, completely. We didn't enroll in school until April, when the marshals moved us into a townhouse in the suburbs of Virginia Beach. My sisters and I were really having a hard time keeping track of all the things we were supposed to remember.

We were told that we couldn't tell anyone that we were from Philadelphia. There were also a few words that we were warned not to utter, words like Muslim and Hanafi. The worst thing of all was that we had to forget our identities, which was very difficult for pre-adolescent children. Mother had become so frustrated with me refusing to answer to our new last name, that she telephoned a federal marshal to come and give me a talking to. The marshal had really angered my sisters and me. He called himself coaching us about information we shouldn't discuss in school. He told us to repeat our new last name silently, about fifty times in order to get used to hearing it. So that if someone calls our names in school, no one would be suspicious, or worse, think we're retarded. I think I was angrier than my sisters about the name change. I was John Jr. My whole identity was wrapped up in being the son of John Sr.

As the marshal continued to coach, my anger began to increase. Suddenly, I shouted, "What are we supposed to say if someone asks us about our father!" The marshal just looked at me as if I were an idiot. Then he said, "John, what do you think I've been talking about for the last twenty minutes?" Then as to give us some absurd Shakespearean lesson, he raised his arms and said, "If someone asks you about your father, you are to deny your father, and deny his name." He told us to deny ever knowing a John Griffin or being related to such a person. He added, "This will keep you all alive." So slowly, we learned to follow the marshal's advice, we denied our father, and denied his name. Even the denouncement of my father's existence wasn't enough to prepare us for the third act of this horrific nightmare. We had begun to finally feel safe with our new identities, only to find ourselves back in the spotlight, trying desperately to hold on to our dirty little secrets.

CHAPTER TWELVE
Dirty Little Secrets

To our pleasant surprise, we returned to Philadelphia on October 12, 1976. We were all exhausted, but mother earned the medal for exhaustion. While we were living under assumed names in Virginia, mother was traveling to Washington, D.C. for father's trial. In his second trial for the Hanafi murders, father caught a break.

On October 5, 1976, Amina Khaalis, survivor of the massacre, testified for the prosecution about father's role in the murders. She had initially identified James Price as the man who pulled her daughter from her arms. Then, at the first trial, she identified father. Then at Ronald Harvey's trial in November 1974, she re-identified James Price as the baby snatcher. Father filed for an immediate appeal, and on January 20, 1975, three weeks after James Price was murdered, the District Court of Appeals granted a new trial. This was a real break for father, because similar to Jerome Sinclair, the government didn't have any physical evidence against him. There were no long distance phone calls made to my father's house on the day before or day after the murders. The only link they had to him was the fugitive flight from prosecution with William Christian, and James Price's testimony about his role in the murders. The crux of the government's case against father depended on two witnesses. The first witness was James Price, who balked at testifying in open court against his co-defendants. The second witness testimony with whom the government now depended on solely was Amina Khaalis.

In the second trial, after the prosecution finished their direct examination of Ms. Khaalis, Dovey Roundtree, father's defense attorney awaited her turn to cross-examine the witness. On the day that the cross-examination was to begin, the court received a letter from Ms. Khaalis' physician. Judge Braman read the letter aloud. The letter detailed a diagnosis of Ms. Khaalis' condition. The physician stated that Ms. Khaalis was emotionally and physically exhausted, after being made to relive the tragic events of her family in court, over and over again. This was the third trial in which Ms. Khaalis was subpoenaed to testify. After Judge Braman read the letter, and excused Ms. Khaalis, Ms. Roundtree requested a mistrial. Ms. Roundtree's argument was sound. She stated that the jury was unduly biased after hearing the one-sided testimony of Ms. Khaalis. She also argued that Ms. Khaalis' failure to be present for cross-examination violated my father's constitutional right to confront his accusers. Although Judge Braman agreed with Ms. Roundtree's argument, he didn't grant the mistrial immediately. He said that he wanted to have Ms. Khaalis' physician testify about her condition before rendering a ruling.

Judge Braman recessed the court until the following day, and issued a subpoena for the Khaalis' physician. When the subpoena was served, the physician refused to come in and testify. This angered Jude Braman, prompting him to issue a bench warrant for the physician, holding him in contempt of court. Finally deciding to avoid a contempt of court charge, Ms. Khaalis' physician came to court to give his testimony. On October 9, 1976, the physician restated everything that had been written in the letter. He told the judge that Ms. Khaalis was under severe stress because of the trials. He also stated that Ms. Khaalis was at risk for having a nervous breakdown if she were to be subjected to further testimony.

On the day of the physician's testimony, a reporter from the Washington Post called Mr. Khaalis and asked him if they would concur with the court order, if Amina were made to testify. Mr. Khaalis told the reporter that he and his family members would resist with their lives any order from the court or anywhere else to make Amina testify. On October 13, 1976, after hearing the physician's testimony, Judge Braman ruled that Ms. Khaalis would not have to come back to court for cross-examination. In the same breath, the judge granted the defense's motion for a mistrial. He granted the motion for mistrial because, as he stated, he didn't believe reasonable people could erase the testimony of Amina Khaalis, identifying my father from their memories.

When Mr. Khaalis heard the news of my father's mistrial, he was livid. He blamed Judge Braman personally, calling him a "Zionist in Satan's Army." Mother, on the other hand, was overjoyed. She was overjoyed because her testimony to corroborate information about Father's involvement was to follow Ms. Khaalis' testimony. Since the mistrial was declared before mother got the opportunity to testify, she felt as if we were somehow spared, and was no longer a threat to the Nation of Islam. So two days after the trial ended, mother, my siblings and I boarded a train at Newport News, Virginia, and headed back to Philadelphia.

The trial not only took a physical and emotional toll on my mother, but on my step-father as well. As we returned home, my step-father decided to stay in Virginia. Their marriage was over. My sisters and I were all so happy to return home to Philadelphia. We thought we'd be reunited with our old friends, our old school, and our old house, but that would not happen. Upon leaving, at the last trial mother was told by the federal prosecutors that they intended to try my father again. They told her that we would continue to be a threat to the Nation of Islam. Mother didn't tell us about a new trial, or anything related to the case, all we knew is that we were coming home.

Since we were not allowed to return to our previous home in Philadelphia, we stayed with our aunt in her apartment. Mother enrolled us in the neighborhood schools a day after our arrival. For my sisters and I this was the most difficult transition, because this was our third school in eight months. My sisters were enrolled at Theodore Roosevelt Junior High School, and I was enrolled at Eleanor Cope Emlen Elementary School.

I was very nervous on the first day at my new school. Once again, I was beginning weeks after school was already in session, and I was a total stranger to everyone in the school. I was assigned to room 408. I was soon over my nervousness, because on the same day I started another student was beginning as well. A pretty little girl named Rebecca Harris.

Prior to meeting Rebecca, I had no real opinion about girls. I had two sisters, but they were sisters. Rebecca was a goddess. She was beautiful, and she was short like me. She had a cocoa tan complexion like my mother, and engaging brown eyes. As Rebecca and I entered class together, the stares and whispers began, but they were not entirely mine to bear, we shared the spotlight. As we stood in front of the classroom, the teacher introduced herself. She said, "I'm Mrs. Jordan, your fourth grade teacher. Please tell us your names." Rebecca went first, then I followed. I said "My name is John Griff….I mean John King." I wanted to kick myself for being so careless. Mrs. Jordan looked at me, and rolled her eyes. I guess she thought I was trying to be funny. With an authoritarian voice, she said, "You and I aren't going to have a problem, are we?" I said, "No, ma'am."

By the time Christmas arrived, I had thoroughly integrated myself into the class. I played, and studied, and loved all in room 408. Football was my game, math was my subject, and Rebecca Harris was the object of my affection. Things seemed to settle down nicely at my aunt's apartment as well. Mother no longer had a look of dread on her face. She even began to date. When we lived in Virginia, mother was going back and forth to Washington for the trial, and my step-father started seeing other women. His cheating had become so bad that one day my sisters and I all stayed home from school, for a teachers' conference, our step-father brought another woman home to our house. He was unaware that we would be home from school, as we usually were gone before he awoke. So on this particular day, when he and the woman decided to come out of mother's bedroom, they were unpleasantly surprised by our presence, as we were by theirs. It was good to see mother moving on with her life. She was still very young and very pretty.

The arrival of 1977 was a peaceful one. It was more peace than any of us had encountered, in more than four years. January and February came and went, without any massacres, jailhouse murders, or federal agents knocking on our door. It seemed as if we were finally out of the woods. Then came Thursday, March 10, 1977.

I remember sitting in the front row, in my assigned seat, waiting anxiously for Mrs. Jordan to call my name, as she was doing roll call. It was career day, and as usual, I was trying mercifully to show Mrs. Jordan that I had dreams of becoming something special. I really didn't have a clue about what I wanted to be at nine years old. The future was too far away to conceptualize anything besides watching "Dr. J" play on court against "The Iceman," or besides hoping to get a kiss from Rebecca. Although I really didn't know what career path I hoped to take, I've always had something in me that made me want to prove myself worthy of adults, especially to teachers. Whenever adults asked, "John, what do you want to be when you grow up?" I would smile and say, either a doctor or a lawyer. I never realized until much later, that the adults asking me those very uncomfortable questions actually asked because they had high expectations for me. This particular day, I wanted to make sure that Mrs. Jordan knew that I wanted to be somebody special.

Mrs. Jordan was very intimidating. She only stood at four feet, eleven inches, and had very thick bifocals, but it seemed that her bifocals had given her x-ray vision. She always seemed to be looking right through me. Since the first day at Emlen, I felt that Mrs. Jordan didn't like me. I guess it started with my clumsy introduction. The same week, she caught me talking in the coat room and slapped my knuckles with a wooden ruler, calling me an evil child. Since that week, I had been trying to show her how good I could be. Mrs. Jordan entered the classroom. Although she spoke very loudly, I didn't hear her. It was as if an airplane was flying directly over our classroom window. I knew neither of those scenarios were occurring. As she walked closer to my direction, I went totally deaf, and my eyes had become a microscope, focusing in on a tiny microorganism. The micro-organism was the newspaper in Mrs. Jordan's hand.

At first focus, all I could see were adjoining pictures of five black men. One of the pictures resembled my father. I closed my eyes for a second, just to be sure that I was not imagining his face. At second glance, I looked at the picture that resembled my father, the man I hadn't seen in four years. "It's got to be him," I whispered to myself. At third glance, I read the caption above the pictures, it read, "Murderers here under tight guard."

Mrs. Jordan seemed to be finishing whatever it was that she was saying, then she walked over to her desk to place the newspaper on top. She began to walk around the room to look at the different things we brought in for Career Day. Finally, regaining full strength of my auditory senses, I heard Mrs. Jordan ask someone behind me to stand up and discuss their career choice. She seemed to be purposely going to the back of the room first, to avoid those of us in the front, whom she repudiated as evil. This was fine with me, because I was shaking like a leaf, thinking about the newspaper. I just knew that my "dirty little secret" had been revealed, and I would become the most hated child in the fourth grade.

There were officially eleven days left in the winter season, and it was freezing cold outside, yet sweat began to pour down my face. I was sweating because I had remembered the lie I told the class a month ago, when Mrs. Jordan asked us to stand up, and tell us about our father's occupations. Some of my classmates said their fathers were sanitation workers, others said security guards, policemen, and others simply didn't know. All I knew is my father was considered to be very dangerous, and that he had been absent from my life for the last four years, so I lied. I told Mrs. Jordan and the class that my father was a congressman in Washington, D.C. Not surprisingly Mrs. Jordan called on me last, even though I was sitting in the middle of the first row. I did what I came to do quite well at that point, I lied. The irony was that I was taught to lie to adults and others, by adults with recognized authority, U.S. Marshals.

When Mrs. Jordan finally called on me, I told the class that I wanted to become an attorney, so that I could eventually go into politics, like my father. Although I was still shaking, I thought my speech was quite convincing. After I spoke, the bell rang for recess.

Mrs. Jordan was herding us out of class so that she could have her coffee in the teachers' lounge, as she did on most occasions. I thought it odd that Mrs. Jordan didn't take her newspaper to read, with her coffee as she normally had. I took advantage of her peculiar behavior by reading the article. I pretended to go to recess with my class, and as soon as the boys' line passed the boys' bathroom, I made my hasty retreat into the bathroom. Then I crept back into my class, to connect the words with the pictures of my father.

Reading the article was a mixed bag. I became both terrified and relieved after reading the article. I was terrified because the article repeatedly referred to my father as a murderer, and not just a murderer but a murderer of children. This was the very first time I had a document that described why my father had been sent to prison. I heard all of the innuendo as early as six years of age, but I was not developmentally equipped to attach any significant meaning to what was being said. This was a terrifying moment. I felt unmasked, vulnerable and guilty. Yes, I also felt guilty, as if by virtue of being the child of an accused murderer that I inherited the indictment. I guess I felt similar to children of divorced parents, who began to blame themselves for their parents' split. Could I have caused his problems with the law? Had he slipped into a life of crime through his escape from the burdens of parenthood? Then the inevitable question: if we were better children, would he have been a better human being?

After these thoughts of terror had subsided, I began to feel relieved. I was relieved because I remembered one very important event; I was no longer John Griffin Jr. This revelation allowed me to feel a sense of disconnect from my father that I desperately needed at that moment. I suddenly began to feel better, and believe that everything would be okay because my "dirty little secret" was still concealed. However, as I continued to read the article the feeling of terror returned, casting a dark shadow over my tiny spirit.

The article read that a few men were holding hostages in three office buildings in Washington, D.C. It also reported that the men were holding the hostages in retaliation to the murders of seven people four years earlier, and they were willing to exchange the hostages or the murderers. The article was a little confusing to me in that it described the hostage takers as Muslims, and also referred to my father and co-conspirators as Muslims.

I knew father was a Muslim. My remaining memories of my father's visits with my sisters and me were pleasant. On several of his visits to our home, he took us to the Temple with him. Some of the Muslim houses of worship were called Temples at the time. My sisters and I would get dressed as the Muslims dressed. Their hair would be wrapped, and I would wear a dark suit and bowtie. We didn't really care for the speeches, there were always lots of speeches, but we enjoyed eating the bean pies that we were sure to receive after the speeches from ministers. The idea that someone would want to harm my father disturbed me profoundly. For the first time I began to think about what the papers were writing about my father. I wanted to know why this terrible thing had occurred. I had feelings of fear and uncertainty about my father's wellbeing. I didn't know if her jailers would turn him over to the hostage takers, and if he would be turned over, if they would murder him for what he was thought to have done to the children in Washington.

When I came home from school, mother was standing in the doorway, waiting for me. I could tell that she had read the paper, because of the look of dread on her face. I had only seen this look on my mother's face on one other memorable occasion. Mother was a very pretty woman. She had a dark cocoa tan complexion, and big brown eyes that resembled Diana Ross. Mother had just celebrated her thirty-first birthday two weeks earlier. Here she stood in the doorway, as if she had the worries of the world imprinted on her brow. When I got to the door, I hugged mother and went inside. I didn't let on that I knew what she apparently knew. Mother began pacing the floor. I remember thinking to myself "Oh no! We must move again." I also remember wishing that everything could be as it was thirteen months earlier, before our lives were turned upside down. If anyone had told my family that we would encounter the ordeals that we have been faced with since February 8th, 1976, we all would have laughed hysterically. Even at nine years of age I knew that turning back the clock was fantasy, we had to face whatever the day was going to bring us, and we did just that. We sat down as a family and watched the third act of the tragedy unfold in front of our eyes.

CHAPTER THIRTEEN
In Harm's Way

As my mother, sisters and I watched the drama unfolding in the nation's capital, a maintenance worker who resided In Washington was living it. March 9, 1977 was an unreasonably warm day. President Carter had only been in office for two months, and he hosted the British Prime Minister at the White House. The people of Washington had long forgotten the Hanafi murders. All of the defendants in the Hanafi saga had been criminally dealt with, with one exception.

Father had been granted a mistrial in his second trial of the Hanafi massacre, after Amina Khaalis' refusal to return to court for cross-examination, due to her emotional condition. Father's first murder trial in Washington was front-page news in the local papers, but the news of the mistrial was buried on the last page of the metropolitan section. To one very important spectator of the Hanafi murder trial, namely Hamaas Khaalis, the ruling was a personal insult.

The court's ruling of a mistrial in my father's case had an injurious effect on Mr. Khaalis, and the lack of priority from the print media in covering the last couple of trials was simply adding insult to injury. At eleven o'clock on that unseasonably warm Wednesday in March, Hamaas Khaalis was preparing to permanently etch his name into the memories of all residents of Washington, D.C., and possibly the world.

Wesley Hymes, a maintenance man for B'nai B'rith, had come into work about eight o'clock that morning, as he did on most days. He worked until about ten forty-five, before preparing to break for an early lunch at eleven o'clock. As Wesley Hymes was grabbing his lunch pail, four men ran into the building that housed the National Headquarters of B'nai B'rith.

The four men were brandishing guns and machetes. The four went on a violent attack upon entering the building, firing off rounds in the air, and pistol-whipping several people in the immediate area, while attempting to round up all of the building's occupants. There were about one hundred people in the building that morning. The four men went floor to floor, swinging their machetes, and firing off more rounds, as they threatened to cut off the heads of those unlucky enough to be in the building. Of the one hundred people inside of the B'nai B'rith building that morning sixty-five became hostages of the four men. Others had heard the fracas and barricaded themselves inside locked offices.

The next strike would occur only an hour later, at an Islamic center. Two men invaded Washington's Islamic center at noon. There were fifteen people in the building at the time of the siege. Seven of the hostages taken inside of the Islamic centers were employees, the other eight were Muslim foreign students. Ironically, the foreign Muslim students were visiting the Islamic center to receive information about their fellow Muslim brothers and sisters, who lived in America. Initially, there was no report of bloodshed at either B'nai B'rith, or at the Islamic center, but the final strike would prove to be deadly.

The third and final strike occurred at the district building, at two-forty in the afternoon. The district building was considered the mecca of city politics. This was where the Mayor's office, and the city council's offices were located. This was also where all city public meetings were conducted. At two-forty, Mayor Walter Washington and most of the city council were in their individual offices on the fifth floor, conducting the city's business. At the same time, two men walked into the district building with shotguns. They took the security guard, who was sitting at the desk on the main floor with them as they rode the elevator up the fifth floor.

As soon as the elevator door opened to the fifth floor, the men pushed the security guard off the elevator. Then they stepped off themselves, and started shooting their shotguns indiscriminately. Maurice Williams, a twenty-four year old news reporter for radio station WHUR, was on the fifth floor corridor, as two men jumped off the elevator. Williams was the first to be hit. He was shot in the back, at point blank range. He cried out, "I'm shot," and died immediately. The bullet that hit Mr. Williams then ricocheted. The ricocheted bullet hit a young city councilman with aspirations to the Mayor's office; that young man was Marion Barry.

Councilman Barry was shot in the chest. He staggered into the city council's chambers, where a hearing was in session. He fell into one of the chairs, shouting "I've been shot." Councilman Barry lost a lot of blood and had to wait about a half hour before any medical help would arrive.

There were two other shootings at the district building. The security guard, who was brought up to the fifth floor with the gunman, was shot in the head, and another building employee was critically wounded. There were many more people in the district building, but like those at the B'nai B'rith building, many barricaded themselves in locked offices to escape the carnage. Mayor Washington's staff locked themselves in his office after hearing the shots in the corridor.

As the police and news reporters began to arrive at the three buildings, the group responsible for the acts, began to stick their heads out of the building windows and to identify themselves, as well as give their reasons for the siege. The group of gunmen at the B'nai B'rith building told a newspaper reporter that they were Hanafi Muslims, and that they were waging a war. The reporter asked why they were waging a war at the three chosen locations. The gunman told the reporter to ask his leader, who was stationed at the district building. The reporter asked the leader's name, and the gunman responded, Khalifa Hamaas Abdul Khaalis.

By three-thirty that afternoon, most of the city's news reporters were in front of the three buildings under siege. At about the same time, a middle-aged black man, wearing black rimmed glasses and a black skull cap with a goatee, emerged in front of one of the windows. The middle-aged man told the reporters that he was the leader, Khalifa Hamaas Abdul Khaalis. According to Khaalis, his group of Hanafi Muslims were waging a war against those who desecrate the true image of Islam.

He told reporters that his war targets particular groups and individuals. First of those being the late Elijah Muhammad's Muslim organization, who he considered responsible for the assassination of Malcolm X, and the massacre of his family. Khaalis' demands were to exchange the hostages in the three buildings for the men convicted of killing his family, so that he could exact his revenge for the killings. He also asked for the men convicted of killing Malcolm X. Individually, he wanted Elijah Muhammad's son, Wallace Deen Muhammad, who was now the leader of the Black Muslims. He also asked for Muhammad Ali. Khaalis never mentioned what he intended to do to either of them, but it was apparent that he blamed them for what happened to Malcolm X and his family.

Wallace Deen Muhammad responded by saying that he had no responsibility for what happened to the Khaalis family. Muhammad Ali refused to comment on the ordeal altogether. Khaalis' last demand was to stop the movie theatres from showing the film, "Muhammad, last messenger of God," which had recently debuted in theatres. Khaalis told reporters that the film depicted Muslims as savages. The film was only showing in New York and Los Angeles. The theatre owners didn't want to be responsible for anyone being killed in the siege, so they honored Khaalis' request. The other message from Khaalis to the reporters had to do with what he intended to do to the hostages if his demands were not honored. He kept repeating from the window, "Heads were gonna roll."

The city of Washington was paralyzed. Upon hearing about the siege, the commerce department closed their offices. The White House decided to halt their nineteen gun salute for the visiting British Prime Minister, because of the close proximity to the buildings. They didn't want to give the gunmen the impression that the police were firing their weapons. Prison officials also tightened up their security on the men accused in the Hanafi killings.

Ronald Harvey was in a jail in Camden County, New Jersey. He was awaiting trial for the murders of Major Coxson and his step-daughter. My father and his co-defendants were placed in isolated cells, at Holmesburg prison. The convicted murderers of Malcolm X were also placed in isolated cells in New York prisons.

The siege went into its thirty-sixth hour, when three ambassadors from the Middle East agreed to go to the district building, to negotiate the release of the hostages. Ashraf Ghorbal of Egypt, Ardeshir Zahedi of Iran, and Sahabzada Yaqubkhan of Pakistan spoke with Hamaas Khaalis via telephone, for three hours. During the three hour conversation, they discussed the Quran, and cited particular verses, hoping to give Khaalis another out from his self-proclaimed war. After speaking with the ambassadors for more than five hours, Khaalis' need for retribution began to wane. However, he felt that he still needed a victory. He didn't want to release the hostages without having received any concessions from city officials.

In the last hour of negotiations with the ambassadors, Khaalis requested that he and his cohorts receive immunity from prosecution, and in return, they would release everyone unharmed. The ambassadors relayed Khaalis' request to Attorney General Griffin Bell, who gave a resounding "no" to the request. Since a man had been killed during the siege, and others critically wounded, there was no way the Attorney General could give the hostage takers immunity from prosecution, even if it meant more deaths. Although immunity from prosecution was out of the question, the law enforcement community was willing to concede something to Hamaas Khaalis.

After hearing that his request for immunity had been turned down, Khaalis asked that he and his associates be released without bail, after their arraignment. The Attorney General was a little apprehensive about agreeing to a no bail release. He was sensitive to how it would look to those in observation of the conflict, to hear of law enforcement bargaining with hostage takers. Then he may have reconsidered because of the imminent consequence of turning Khaalis down on yet another request. He may have imagined the decapitated heads rolling out of windows, ordered by a man who had nothing else to lose.

The Attorney General took the offer to D.C. Superior court judge, Harold Greene, who agreed with the Attorney General Bell's rationale. Then, the ambassadors relayed Attorney General Bell's conditions for the agreement to Khaalis. The conditions were that Hamaas Khaalis and his associates could not leave city limits, and must turn in their passports at the arraignment hearing. Khaalis agreed to the conditions and released all hostages at two o'clock in the morning, on Friday, March 11, 1977.

Upon release of the hostages, Khaalis and his associates were arrested immediately. Twelve men in total were arraigned in district court on that Friday morning. All but two men were released without bail. The two held were not released because they were identified as the men who fired the fatal shot that killed Maurice Williams and wounded Councilman Marion Barry.

Some groups that had come to Washington to monitor the hostage drama were disturbed by the release of Khaalis and the others. One group in particular was determined to send their own message of war to anyone within earshot of the Hanafi compound.

The Jewish Defense League, who came mainly from Brooklyn and Philadelphia, decided to pay the Hanafis a visit. Rabbi Meir Kahane, and his followers arrived in Washington a few days after the siege. Armed with machetes of their own, the JDL headed to the home of Hamaas Khaalis. There were about one hundred members of the JDL in front of the Hanafi compound. They began their protest of the Hanafis by chanting, "Allah is dead, and we want Khaalis, we want him dead."

The police arrived and attempted to break up the demonstration, or at least contain it. As the police presence grew stronger, members of the JDL began to pass out baseball bats. As the bats were passed, members began shouting, "Remember the King David hotel."

The King David hotel was a reference to the 1946 bombing at the hotel in Jerusalem by an underground Zionist group. Ninety people were killed in the bombing. Then they chanted, "Auschwitz, Dachau, never again, and be a jew-.22!" Rabbi Kahane shouted, "I want every Jew with a .22, and know how to use it." After a few hours of the protest at the Hanafi compound, the JDL were escorted by the police to the airports. The Khaalis' never once opened a curtain, or went outside during the JDL's protest.

On May 31, 1977, two months after the siege, Hamaas Khaalis and eleven co-defendants went on trial. They were all charged with conspiracy, multiple counts of armed kidnapping, as well as a second degree charge of murder, in the death of Maurice Williams. The trial lasted twelve weeks, and on July 24th, a jury of two men and ten women brought back twelve verdicts of guilty for each Hanafi member.

Hamaas Khaalis, who was now fifty-five years old, was convicted of second degree murder, conspiracy and armed kidnapping. Upon sentencing, Khaalis would receive a life sentence. The same sentence that he had hoped would be given to the murderers of his family. As the Khaalis trial came to a close, the last trial involving the Hanafi murders was about to begin.

In August of 1977, mother received the call that we all had been dreading. All of us knew that the federal marshals would be darkening our doorstep once again, after we heard that the federal prosecutors were preparing for father's third trial. The prosecutors had previously warned mother that if they were unsuccessful prosecuting my father in the last case, they would try until they got a conviction. So we knew that we were living on borrowed time.

Just as we were reading about the conclusions in Hamaas Khaalis' trial, mother received the dreaded call. The marshal told my mother that the federal prosecutors wanted her testimony at trial, and that they were instructed to come and move us again, because we were no longer safe. Our safety seemed to coincide with the prosecutors' need for mother's testimony. The call was the same, as was the message; we needed protection, because we were in harm's way.

On October 4, 1977, a week before father's third trial was to begin, we moved. This was our third move in twenty months. This was also my sister Dana's thirteenth birthday. We had just begun a new school year three weeks earlier. I was in the fifth grade, my last year in elementary school. My sister Darshell, was in the seventh grade, and Dana, who had just become a teenager, was in her last year of junior high school. The very thought of moving again was very difficult for all of us, but it was especially difficult for Dana, and our younger brother Larry, who was only three years old.

Dana and Larry were at opposite poles of child development. Dana was pretty and tall, but the average awkward teenager. She was enjoying the social benefits of being in the final year of junior high school. Dana was a great athlete, who flourished in softball. She also contemplated auditioning for the cheerleading squad at her school, when we received the call to start packing. At the other end of the spectrum was our most vulnerable sibling, my baby brother Larry.

Larry was just a toddler, and was getting over his first bout of separation anxiety, suffered when mother left for the last trial. Larry was really attached to mother. When she went to testify last year, he stayed with our aunt. Larry sobbed for mother every day; he was heartbroken. Her absence had such a traumatic effect on him that when mother returned from the last trial, Larry would wrap his arms around mother's leg and refuse to let her leave him to go anywhere. Mother couldn't even go to the bathroom without him.

The federal marshals arrived at our apartment at nine o'clock in the morning. They must have been new to the case, because I didn't recognize any of them. We had become accustomed to seeing the first two marshals, who had initially come to our house during the first move. These marshals appeared younger, and both were tall with dark hair. They looked to be younger than mother, in their early twenties. One of the marshals handed my mother an envelope, and informed her that there was some cash enclosed with the location of the new house.

Mother seemed a little hesitant, and asked the marshal why we had to move. With this being father's third trial in Washington, mother figured that it shouldn't take longer than a month. So she asked if she could leave us with relatives, as not to disturb our education, while she testified. The marshal told my mother that he was under direct orders from the U.S. Attorney, and the F.B.I. to move all of us. Then he went to explain to mother why we all needed to be together.

He said, "Ma'am, we were told by the prosecutor in your ex-husband's case that things may get a little dangerous for anyone who testifies in this case." He told mother about the other cases he covered, involving mobsters. He mentioned Jimmy "the weasel" Fratiani, and the threats against his family, due to his testimony. He also mentioned a retired mafia boss from Chicago named Sam Giancana. Giancana was recently found murdered in his home, a day before he was to testify before a grand jury. Mother was baffled by the marshals stroll down Mafioso memory lane. She told him, "We are not Italian, nor am I testifying against an organized crime syndicate." The marshal told mother that she didn't have to be Italian, or testifying against La Costra Nostra, and then he reminded mother of the title given to father's associates by the local police and news media;The Black Mafia.

He explained to mother that he knew nothing about black organized crime, but he knew what he heard from senior agents, who believed that the Philadelphia chapter of the Black Muslims were involved in organized criminal activity. In his attempt to scare mother further, the marshal told mother about an informant. The informant apparently told the F.B.I. that he was propositioned to execute a contract on our lives.

Mother screamed, "Why!" The marshal said, somehow the word had gotten out to the leadership in the Nation of Islam that father had decided to cut a deal with the prosecutors in exchange for his testimony about who gave the order for the massacre. Mother looked at the marshal in total disbelief. Then rolling her eyes, mother said, "Then if you believe that to be the case, what the hell do you need me in Washington to testify if you've got him to cut a deal?" Grinning, the marshal said, "I didn't say the scenario was true, I just said that's what the Muslim leaders were told." Anger was very visible on mother's face. She realized that the prosecutors were using us as pawns.

The next day, we were living in an apartment in Randallstown, Maryland. Mother swiftly enrolled us into the local schools, to ensure that we wouldn't have any long gaps in our school attendance. As much as my sisters and I wanted to hate our new home, we couldn't. Randallstown was a beautiful, peaceful little suburb, right outside of Baltimore. Our apartment was as large as any of the houses we occupied. We had three large bedrooms, and two full bathrooms, with a patio. Our schools were nice, and we met friends immediately, unlike in Virginia. We thought we'd be the only blacks in the school, as we were in Virginia, but to our pleasant surprise there were many blacks living in Randallstown. The evening after we returned from our first day of school, mother called us in for a family meeting. She sat us down and informed us of her plans. She told us that since the federal marshals saw it fit to use her for the trial, she had decided to keep us in Randallstown, even after the trial. Mother said the only reason that would make us move again, would be for reasons of real threats against our lives. This told me that mother really began to doubt whether any of the threats against us were real, or created as a scare tactic by the F.B.I. to coerce mother to testify. Mother said since we were still officially a part of the Witness Protection Program, she would have to clear our stay with the F.B.I. when the trial was over, but she was sure that they would agree, unless there was real and imminent danger. My sisters and I were not fully convinced that the government was going to allow us to stay, especially if it didn't suit their purpose.

Father's third trial began on October 11, 1977. Everything about the third trial was different. The most visible difference was the lack of press coverage. Since the Hanafi siege of the three buildings in March, and the subsequent trial convictions of the twelve in July, the press had shifted its interest of coverage. At this trial, the prosecution's witness list had also changed dramatically.

Almina Khaalis, who reportedly was on the verge of a nervous breakdown at father's second trial, was no longer listed as a witness. The prosecution would be trying the case this time without eyewitness testimony, but they did read Almina's testimony from the first trial. The prosecution also had the testimony of investigating detectives and forensic experts to support their case. They also had the testimony of two former wives of the Hanafi murder defendants--James Price's widow and my mother.

After the detectives testified, mother was called to the stand. Mother was asked to recall a phone conversation she had with father, a week after the Hanafis were murdered. She testified that father had phoned her to ask about getting us for the weekend. She told him that we were going to her sister's, but he could get us the following weekend. Then being the curious person she is, she asked father if he had read the newspaper article in yesterday's paper. Apparently, a wire story from Washington was written a few days after the murder, linking weapons stolen at a party in Philadelphia to the murders. Mother testified that when she asked father if he thought the newspaper article was true, he allegedly commented that the weapons from the Philadelphia house were not used in the murders. After my mother's testimony, the prosecution called James Price's widow to the stand. She testified that father and his co-defendants were at her house planning the retaliation against Khaalis for the letter. After Mrs. Price's testimony, the prosecution rested its case.

Dovey Roundtree, father's lead defense counsel, began her cross-examination of both mother and Mrs. Price. She attempted to reduce their testimony to simply hearsay, painted up by the prosecution, to fix their broken case. Ms. Roundtree's argument was that the government offered no tangible evidence, placing father in Washington on the day of the murders. She contended that the federal government was attempting to convict father on the basis of mass circumstantial evidence, and physical evidence that may have implicated others, but not father.

The only link the prosecution had to possibly connect father in the killings was his fugitive flight with William Christian to Florida, and James Price's grand jury testimony. Since Price was dead, and the flight from prosecution in and of itself, was not enough to sustain the government's burden of proof, the prosecution case was pretty weak. I guess that's why they felt they needed James Price's widow and mother.

The trial lasted three weeks, with Mrs. Price and mother's testimony being a moot point, without eyewitness testimony. A jury deliberated for three days, before rendering a verdict of not guilty. Father was acquitted on all charges relating to the Hanafi murders, and with the double jeopardy clause, this time prosecutors could not try him again.

The day after the trial ended, one of the very few reporters covering the story raised a very important question. He wondered if there hadn't been a siege, and a killing by the Hanafis, if a jury would have had more sympathy for the massacre, and voted for a conviction instead, or was John Griffin simply innocent. Whatever the outcome, mother was relieved that her role in it was finished.

Mother returned home, with a large weight removed from her shoulders. She had done what was asked of her. She had suffered a failed marriage, and compromised a bond with her youngest child, due to her absence for the trial. Mother was now ready to reclaim her family, and enjoy her life in Randallstown.

In December 1977, only three weeks after the trial ended, and three weeks before Christmas, mother phoned the marshals in a panic. She hadn't received any money from the program since the trial had ended. She even phoned F.B.I. headquarters, frantically hoping to speak with someone who handled her case in the Witness program. On December 10th, with our rent a month past due, a marshal finally returned mother's call.

Mother asked why she hadn't received a stipend for December. Responding in a cavalier fashion, the marshal said that they had determined that we were no longer in danger, therefore we didn't require any further protection from the program. Then he told mother that they wished us much success and that she would receive a termination in the mail. Mother was without words, she didn't know how to respond, so she didn't. She simply hung up the phone.

Mother didn't have the opportunity to look for work in Randallstown because of the trial. She was in Washington every day, during every session of the trial. She knew the government was using us as pawns, when they had revealed the false information that was allegedly sent to the Muslims. Mother wasn't a stupid woman, she knew that there was no way to get out of testifying, especially after hearing about the planted, false information. Mother thought the government would at least honor their promise, or even live up to their end of the bargain, especially since she had lived up to her agreement to testify. But they didn't live up to anything.

The Witness Protection Program, under the auspices of the Justice Department, had used us like someone uses a Kleenex. They had soiled our name, calling mother a material witness. They had moved us away from the Muslim "boogeymen," three times in twenty months. They told us that we were in harm's way, when they were the ones putting us in harm's way by leaking false information. Finally, after soiling us with death threats and other false information, they threw us away without so much as bus fare back to Philadelphia.

We were in a dire situation, and mother had no choice but to call her family in Philadelphia to send us bus fare to get back home, because we had no money to keep the apartment. We didn't even have money to send our furniture back to Philadelphia, so we left everything in Randallstown. We returned to Philadelphia on a Greyhound bus two days before Christmas.

No one was more upset about the government's disregard for my family than I. I had even envisioned myself as an F.B.I. agent, after believing that they sincerely cared about the welfare of my family. I really felt let down. I felt disdain, their contempt for my family, and I also felt guilty for believing some of the things that the marshals said about my father. They had described him as a monster, someone who should be shunned. We were told to deny him, and his name. We obliged the request.

On the bus ride home, I thought about many things. I was only ten years old, yet I felt like an adult. I had been privy to such horrific information that no ten year old should have to encounter. I had been asked to forget my identity, lie about my past, and protect my mother and sisters. One of the other things that resonated on that fateful bus ride home was the idea of racism. I wondered if our contemptible treatment by the government had to do with us being a black family, possibly the first black family in the program. I wondered about it, and it made me sick to my stomach. Later, I would read many stories and watch a couple dozen films about the tribulations of people and families in the Witness Protection Program, but the people discussed were always white.

I must say that the government's treatment of my family served as the impetus for my curiosity about this case, and the state of blacks at the hands of the Justice Department. Had it not been for their contempt for us, I would have never wandered into the library to research this case, nor would it have prepared me for the lessons I was about to learn about myself and my father.

CHAPTER FOURTEEN
In the Shadow of the Thin Man

In my adolescent desperation to understand my father, I ventured into an apprenticeship program for the sons of hustlers. I began my first year of high school with my best friend Jimmy. Jimmy, who was six months older than myself, was considered to be Black Mafia royalty. Jimmy's father, who was also incarcerated, was also a part of the 1970's era Black Mafia.

His father, Little Billy, was a heroin dealer, serving a sentence of 5 to 10 for manslaughter. Jimmy's father had come from South Philadelphia, where the Italian Mafia was located. The South Philadelphia arm of the Black Mafia was held in higher esteem among criminals and gangster groupies. The South Philly guys were considered the moneymakers. They were the extorters and drug traffickers. They also had the ear of the Italian Mob Family run by Angelo Bruno. In contrast the North and West Philadelphia arm of the Black Mafia consisted of strong arm and stick-up men.

Jimmy and I had begun high school in the fall of 1981, the year of the long teacher's strike that lasted almost 60 days. In retrospect, I search for reasons as to why I think I gravitated to be with a group of hustlers. I was a sensitive, quasi-athletic, short child, who was considered to be partly nerdy because of my grammatical skills. For the most part, I was also a loner, who deplored violence and cheating of any kind, except in practical jokes.

I recall four years earlier, when my mother sent me to buy a newspaper from a newspaper machine. A woman stood behind me as I inserted my coins in the machine to open it. As I reached for the paper, she grabbed the door and took a paper without putting her coins in the machine. I was so mad that I cried when I got home. I was always fundamentally a fair child, and it really upset me that someone would cheat.

Fast forward to my association with the so-called hustlers of Germantown. So here I am with mafia royalty on the first day of school; it was about 28 degrees Fahrenheit and Jimmy's decked out in a black leather jacket with a hooded fox fur collar. He had on red custom made slacks from the tailor, Joseph Palmieri, who created these ghetto chic slacks without waistbands. Jimmy was also wearing black lizard shoes. This was the style that many of the older hustlers in Philadelphia had embraced in the late 1970's to early 1980's. Italian slacks, colorful stripe printed shirts by a designer called "GENO," and reptile shoes. Jimmy's whole outfit had cost him about $800.0, which was a lot of money in 1981 for a fourteen-year-old. Many of the freshman, myself included, were envious of Jimmy's style, charm with the young ladies, and his ability to socialize with the seniors.

Germantown High School seemed to be a breeding ground for children of the Black Mafia. Since Germantown was the high school located closest to the black working/middle class area known as Mount Airy, many first generation "Mount Airyeans," whose parents either worked or hustled their way up out of the slums of North, South, and West Philly, found themselves in attendance at Germantown High. Most of the first generation "Mount Airyeans" who attended Germantown were below average students, but were ironically considered "uppity" by those left behind who attended high schools in the poorer sections of the city.

I had never felt so alone as I did in my first year in high school, until I met so many sons and daughters of Black Mafia figures in that year that we could have started our own game show titled, "What's my dad's line?" Some of the guys who were indicted in the heroin roundup of 1974-75 had kids at the high school.

The only hustling that went on in Germantown was really from student to student. We would play craps in the bathroom and in the schoolyard, hoping to win a few dollars off of a fellow class-mate. At least that was the extent of my hustling. Other guys within the circle were a little bolder. Jimmy and some of the others, were not only some of the best dice shooters I have ever observed, mainly because they cheated, but they were also drug dealers. Jimmy sold marijuana since we were in the 8ᵗʰ grade, in junior high. He was pretty good at it too. He would purchase an ounce of weed for about sixty five dollars, and roll about eighty five to ninety joints. He would make about thirty-five dollars off of each ounce he purchased, which was money to those of us who had never worked, or received any allowance. Other guys robbed houses in the neighborhood, and still others had part-time jobs after school, but lied about the job to make it look as if they were earning the money illegally.

Even within the circle of hustlers, I felt like an outsider. It was a pretty vicious group in their selection of members. I knew I was really only tolerated because of my association with Jimmy. I was one of the poorer kids at Germantown. My mother didn't have the money to buy me any of the clothes most of my classmates were wearing, so I was judged harshly for not having the latest fashion wears like my friend Jimmy. I was short and dark, so not only was I not in the running for the "pretty-boy" category, I was also out of the "tough guy" competition. Had it not been for Jimmy, I would have been a complete loner that year.

It was a vicious initiation into the circle; the guys were rather cruel to me because as far as they were concerned, I didn't have the credentials to be in their inner circle. As the months grew, my membership was getting shakier and shakier. Jimmy had only introduced me as his friend, which gave me an introduction but didn't ensure my continued stay. It was analogous to admission to a college. If you didn't have your own reputation or credentials to get in, you had to go the "legacy" route. Jimmy not only had his own reputation, but he had the reputation of Little Billy, who was a legend in the underworld of South Philadelphia. The only thing I really knew about the Black Mafia at the time was what I had overheard in adult conversations.

They were a group of men, who had imitated the practices and behaviors of the well-recognized Italian mafia. Unfortunately, my self-esteem was at a pretty low point in high school, and I felt like I needed to belong somewhere, or I would have just evaporated into the landscape. In my desperation for validation from the so-called hustlers, I did an unforgivable thing. I violated one of my family's most guarded secrets. I talked about my father.

For at least five years, no one spoke about my father, not about his whereabouts, his status, nothing. My siblings and I were literally debriefed about any knowledge concerning our biological father. I had vowed to my mother, my siblings and also to myself to never discuss information concerning father. However, my desperation at Germantown forced me to re-think my promise. My father's criminal activity and his associates were legends. I figured disclosing who I was to my peers would have made it impossible for them not to accept me as one of them. What I didn't realize was that since I hadn't talked about him for such a long time, I had forgotten a lot. So I was forced to sit down and think about what I actually knew of the man I called my father.

The two memories that came to me immediately were bittersweet. My first memory was of my last encounter with my father. He had come over to see me and take me with him for the day. Father had taken me to a house with some of his male friends, who were all dressed in suits. They almost resembled a singing group because they were all tall and thin, at least that's how they looked to me at five years of age. I remember my father got compliments about me from his friends, which was in direct contrast to my last memory.

The last memory I had occurred when I was four years of age, and it's much more vivid in my mind. My father came by one evening to visit my sisters and me. I remember sitting in the dining room as he walked into the house. The first thing he did was to grab my hands. One of my sisters had decided to put nail polish on my fingernails, or I had done it myself in imitation of the women in the house. Father was noticeably angry at the sight of his eldest son wearing nail polish. He admonished me for the display, telling me that he never wanted to see it on my hands again. I remember feeling bad about the whole episode. I saw him so infrequently that I didn't want to give him any reason to stop coming to visit me.

I realized that other than two very dramatic dates that were entrenched in my psyche, I only had those very young memories of my father. It was almost ironic, but my desire to be with the "undesirables" led me to the library. I remembered hearing that the main public library kept old newspaper articles on microfiche, so I got my bus tokens together and went to the library. I asked all kinds of questions of those at the reference desk about using the microfiche machine to locate the news articles. After about a week of questions, I was an old pro. I had become quite self-sufficient, and had also begun to enjoy the process of looking for information.

I began to copy the newspaper articles and bring them to school as proof that I belonged with the tough guys, the hustlers. The word soon circulated that I was as connected to the Black Mafia as Jimmy, and soon after, I was asked all kinds of questions about my father. I wish I had observed a very sage piece of wisdom, "To whom much is given, much is required." Since I was now in the "family," I was asked to perform certain tasks that went with being a part of the inner circle.

I also began to take on the persona of a hustler. I became more aware of what I wore to school. All of a sudden the clothes my mother managed to buy for me from her limited income were no longer good enough. Like Jimmy, I wanted to get my nails manicured, and my hair cut weekly. I wanted to shop downtown for my shoes at the exclusive shops like Bootega, Cote'd'azur, and LaStrega. I also wanted to purchase jewelry. However, for me, this would be almost impossible. My mother worked a full time job, supporting my two sisters, my brother, and me. She had no money to give me, and I was too young to get working papers to work legally. If I really wanted these things, there was only one other option, to hustle.

Jimmy became pretty adept to hustling through his selling of reefers. He wouldn't spend any of the profit. He would keep "flippin the package" until he had enough to buy a half-ounce or an ounce. Jimmy did this all summer. That's how he was able to buy the leather jacket with the fox fur collar. In fact, he was the first kid that I ever saw carrying around fifty dollar bills. After watching my best friend earn enough money to buy his own clothes and earn the respect of the older guys in the neighborhood. I decided that it was time for me to get into the business.

In our freshmen year, the public transportation system introduced bus transpasses that a rider would purchase Sunday for a week of rides without interruption. They introduced this unique card at $6.50. The passes were distributed throughout the city high schools for students to purchase, since we were the majority of the bus authority's business. Somehow one of Jimmy's classmates intercepted a delivery between the delivery trucks to the school. Jimmy got his hands on 200 bus transpasses selling at $6.50 a pass. This was my debut to the game of hustling. Jimmy gave me 100 passes to sell at a discounted rate of $5.00. I was to kick him back $250.00. The passes were selling like hotcakes. I would stand at the bus stops when we got out of school and let everyone know what I had. I sold about 45 passes in one hour. One of my classmates thought he deserved a better discount than we offered, so he snitched on me to the disciplinary dean.

I was summoned to the dean's office the next day with two passes on my person. The dean was going to have me arrested, but I told him that I had purchased the passes hot like everyone else. I told him that I purchased two, one for me, and one for my sister. He didn't believe me. He requested that I return to his office the next day with the identification of the person who sold me the passes. I knew that he couldn't have me arrested for the incident, so I balked. I had only sold half of the passes since my business was interrupted, but I had profited $125.00 from the deal. So with my newfound wealth I purchased two and a half ounces of marijuana and decided to go into business.

I wasn't quite the pharmaceutical entrepreneur that Jimmy was. It took me too long to unload the stuff, and I found myself spending the profit before I could get a full account of what I actually made. Although I wasn't making much money, I enjoyed being identified as a hustler, and being in the company of other hustlers. Jimmy and I had changed our first names to Arabic names and I began to attend the Mosque's congregational prayer on Fridays.

We were so enamored with the image that Islam represented to us. Never mind that people who truly believed in their faith were there to pray; we were there to be seen. Most of us who attempted to read the Quran didn't understand what we were reading, nor did we seek the understandings of those who were knowledgeable. It was all about image. Islam represented a coolness, and brotherhood for the hustler in Philadelphia, to mock and use as a shield for protection. Though my days in the drug trade were short lived, my inaccurate and downright ignorant concept of Islam lasted too long for me to admit. The blissful ignorance of my understanding of Islam would send me to the library once again, for information about the religion, and also about my father. Soon my ignorance would turn me from a hustler to a detective, and my misunderstandings would turn into revelations.

CHAPTER FIFTEEN
Revelations

What began as an innocent, nonchalant curiosity about my father's past blossomed into an occupational compulsive search into a child's nightmare. After being knighted, and red-carpeted into the status of Black Mafia royalty by high school cronies, I decided to return to the library with the hopes of finding more articles on my father - the legend.

To my delight, the main public library had a wealth of information about what put most of the men from my father's era in prison. I immediately requested the newspaper dated March 10, 1977 because that was the beginning of my consciousness into my father's notoriety. Simultaneously, I began to receive letters on a regular basis from my father, who was at the time, incarcerated at a federal penitentiary in Marion, Illinois.

Marion's prison was considered the "Alcatraz" of the new era because of its hard line structure. The inmates were locked down in their cells twenty-three hours a day. They were only let out an hour a day for exercise and a shower. This seemed to be cruel and unusual punishment for me.

My father arrived at Marion in 1980, after serving two years in Atlanta's federal prison. While in Atlanta, my father was reacquainted with a few members from the Philadelphia's Black Mafia. Bo Baynes and Russell Barnes were both sent to prison after being convicted of heroin distribution in 1975. Both Baynes and Barnes were sentenced to fifteen years in prison. Russell Barnes would be released in 1985 only to be murdered eight months later in an attempt to take control of the heroin operation that was being run by his rival, Jackie Wright. Bo Baynes would serve the entire 15 year sentence. When he returned to the streets, he opened a very successful restaurant. This connection with influential mafia members in Atlanta allowed my father to hire an attorney.

In his last year in Atlanta, he began to write very optimistic letters to his children about returning home within a couple of years. I remember my sister wrote our father, asking him if he thought he would be home by the time she graduated from high school. My father responded, "a resounding yes." My sister graduated high school in 1982, without pomp and circumstance, and without father.

In late 1982, my father sent me a letter that seemed to be the answer to his dreams, and my own. He was getting transferred to Pennsylvania. My father sounded so happy in his letter to finally be coming close to home. He and I were becoming very close via the mail. I was almost sixteen. I hadn't seen him face to face in ten years, and I really wanted to get to know him. I wanted to replace those very bittersweet memories I had of him, with a real bond. I didn't want to know him through a newspaper article, but really know him. I really wanted to get to know this man that all my friends thought deserved so much respect.

In June 1983, a few days after my sixteenth birthday, and his 38th birthday, my father arrived at Graterford State Penitentiary. At age sixteen I felt like an ugly duckling. I weighed only one hundred pounds; and I only stood at five feet three inches. I was awkward, skinny, and short. On the first of many visits to Graterford to see my father, my two sisters accompanied me. We were all seeing our father for the first time in a decade. This was our first time visiting anyone in prison, let alone our father.

The procedures seemed arduous, and we seemed to wait forever before we would get that first glimpse of our father, the legend. Everything that I felt about myself at the time, my father indirectly confirmed. I was awkward, skinny, short and ugly.

My father was the complete opposite; he was suave, graceful, thin, tall, and had a full mustache. He was very handsome. My sisters and I were in awe of my father. He had a presence that one couldn't ignore. When he walked into the visiting room women and men alike would immediately stop their conversations and look up to take notice of this rare prison specimen. I lived vicariously through father's charm that summer, and felt his power over other inmates and myself, on many of those visits to the prison. So many of those early visits presented me with ambivalent feelings of awkwardness and charm.

As we grew closer, father began to recruit me into his agenda. He had sized me up at this point. He knew through my conversations that I was hanging with the hustlers, and he seemed to approve. He often spoke of his desire to return to the streets, and how with a little bit of capital, he could ensure his return with the right attorney. I had bragged to father that I had sold marijuana, and had earned enough to pay for clothes. Father's response was interesting. If you are going to hustle, hustle for something worthwhile. In that poetic statement was a hidden message that just went over my head, but I got it on the second try. If you are going to hustle, hustle to get your father out of jail.

From that point, father and I became partners. Thanks to the generosity of family, father put together enough money to purchase a half pound of marijuana. My job was to pick up the weed, and take it to its final place for distribution, the state prison.

I took a lot of chances with the hustlers in high schools, but the greatest chances I have ever undertaken were to bring contraband (drugs) to the prison on a regular basis. I was seventeen years old at this point, yet I was taking risks that most adults wouldn't think of doing.

Since we didn't have a vehicle, I would purchase a seat to ride on one of the van services that brought relatives of prisoners up to see them. Most of the Pennsylvania prisons are located upstate, at least an hour away from Philadelphia. So, in order to see your loved ones, you had to spend anywhere from ten to fifteen dollars for a roundtrip on a crowded van.

I would literally have a bulk of weed stuffed under my shirt as I walked from the van to the prison. Then I would go into the men's bathroom inside of the prison's main waiting room, where visitors were kept until being sent to the visiting room, and wait for my contact. My contact, the person who took the contraband from me and got it inside the prison, was a guy who worked on the outside of the prison, but was still a prisoner. The contact would take the weed from me in the bathroom, and for about the cost of an ounce (which was about $100 in prison, and only $45 to $50 on the street) he would take the weed inside.

This relationship of distributing contraband (marijuana) went on with my father and me for more than a year. I felt closer to him because of our business relationship, and I really felt like I was helping him. In hindsight, I think I was always trying to compensate for disappointing him with the nail-polish when I was four years old.

I even mentioned my memory of the nail-polish event to my father on one of my visits, and I guess since we were partners, father felt comfortable disclosing his feelings about me at that time. I guess he figured since I was a big time hustler, a tough guy, I could handle whatever he said. My father, who I hadn't seen in a decade whom I had become mixed up with in the distribution of drugs to prison inmates, basically told me that he was ashamed when he saw the polish on my nails, and thought I was weak and becoming a "sissy." He also said that he was that much more elated by the news that his current wife was pregnant with a son, because this son who would have been raised by him would be tough. He actually told me that he had my half-brother to replace me.

Although I didn't show it, I was crushed. I couldn't believe that my own father could have so much contempt for his own child as to want to replace him. He actually thought of me as some "sissy." Suddenly, my need to be affiliated with the tough guys at school made sense. Everything I had engaged in as a teenager began to make sense. I was living in my father's shadow. I was attempting to emulate someone, who really didn't think much of me until I began to exhibit his behaviors.

Father's revelation didn't make me sever the relationship; in fact, it drew me closer. Oddly enough, I felt a stronger desire to know this man. He became an enigma to me, almost like an anecdote to a horrible disease. I desperately needed to know why my father was really where he was.

The newspapers gave me headlines, but it didn't allow me to know if my father was really the monster they described him to be. More of our visit discussions were centered on his criminal cases. Father would speak at length about his cases, but there was always this sense that he was holding something back. I didn't know if he was holding back to protect me, or if he didn't think I could handle it, which seemed ridiculous since he thought I could partner with him in the trafficking of drugs to the prison. The only other option was that he thought he couldn't trust me with the information.

One of the things I learned researching articles about my father in the library came from one of the librarians at the reference desk. I had begun my search looking at the articles from one newspaper. The librarian noticed this and told me to check every available newspaper. He said "Never trust a story coming from only one source." That advice stayed with me, even as I listened to my father's explanation as to why he was incarcerated.

When I turned eighteen I gave up all of my illegal hustling and settled for a regular job. I began working at the Veteran's Affairs office in the city, but continued to help my father as much as I could with his defense. I had all the information on his case that I was going to find in the newspaper, so I began checking out some other sources. I began going to the courthouse for anything I could find on father's case. I began looking at his actual criminal folder for information about his arrests. It was very confusing at first, because when you go to look up someone's criminal record, either their prison number that they use while incarcerated is the same number on their file, or simply the person's name and date of birth becomes the reference in looking up their information. In my father's cases, there were two district numbers. I didn't learn until much later, that one represented his state arrest and convictions. The other represented his federal arrest and convictions.

The state arrests were easier to read, but the federal cases proved a little more difficult. It led me to the James Byrne Federal courthouse in Philadelphia, which must have been a godsend because when I looked up father's information, there was a name that kept recurring. It was the name of an attorney in Washington, who wasn't a lead attorney in charge of the particular federal case, but had worked very closely on the case.

My detective work was cut short due to my lack of funds. The latter part of my eighteenth year, I enlisted in the Army. I needed to get out of my environment as I was drifting back into the life of criminal activity, and I desperately did not want to end up in prison with my father.

After my three-year stint, I returned home with a new sense of direction and purpose. The following year, I enrolled in college. I also continued to visit my father when the time allowed. I was no longer in his shadow, but creating my own. I was twenty-two years old, and had somehow become an individual. I was happy with my individuality, but continued to fill the need for closure with my respect to feelings of guilt and insecurity about my father. The attorney whose name continuously came up on my father's federal file had once again invaded my mind. I wanted to know what had happened to my father, and what had happened to any of the victims connected to his case. I summoned the courage after looking at his name on my bureau for six months.

I called the Metropolitan Washington area, hoping to find this attorney. To my surprise, she was still in practice, with just a year to go to her retirement. I immediately purchased a train ticket, and went down to Washington, D.C. I must have looked like a lost child to this attorney. I came into her office with my hands shaking, asking if she could help me find information on this old case that had been long solved and closed to all of the players in Washington. She asked me what my purpose for obtaining the information was, and I attempted to lie, telling her that it was for an assignment at college. Instead, I decided to tell the truth. I told her that I was a son, trying desperately to find out what happened to my father. The attorney understood. She excused herself, and came back into her office about forty-five minutes later with a stack of folders. She told me that none of the folders could leave her office, but I was welcomed to look at everything she had and take notes. I did just that, I read and I took lots of notes.

The picture I got from reading the case, and the police reports were extremely different from some of the stories I read in the newspaper, and some of the stories from my father. I spent several weeks in Washington, trying to pull all of the pieces together. There are still some pieces missing from my research, such as identifying the individual(s) who gave the order to send men to Washington to kill the Khaalis'. Since no one else has ever spoken publicly about the case, and the government's alleged witness was murdered, there is that possibility that we may never know who actually gave the order. The other missing piece has to do with my own father, the only individual who was tried three times in the Hanafi murders, and the only suspect in the case to be acquitted.

My father has proclaimed his innocence in this case for over twenty years, and has also proclaimed his innocence in the murder of James Price. Father believes that the prosecutors, angry about not being able to keep their initial conviction to him, decided to frame him for the Price murder with a jailhouse informant who cut a deal with the Philadelphia prosecutors, who were cooperating with the federal prosecutors.

Having a clearer understanding of "COINTELPRO" (the F.B.I.'s counter intelligence program) and what possibly happened in the assassination of some of the sixties leaders, my father's theory doesn't seem so far off the mark. If his assertions were correct, then James Price would have had to be what is known as an "agent provocateur." An "agent provocateur" describes an individual who, under auspices of law enforcement, joins an organization with the sole purpose of spying and creating confusion/wrecking havoc within the organization. Today, we know that there were many people in the traditional Civil Rights and Black Power Organizations who were serving the function of an "agent provocateur."

The problem with this theory is that it takes the responsibility off of the actual offenders. If there is collusion with the federal government in a sanctioned murder of Black people, all parties need to be made responsible, sharing equally in the commission of the act. I'm afraid that we will never know fully how many people, or which people were involved. However it adds up, it was unnecessary. In fact, it was an unnecessary evil.

CHAPTER SIXTEEN
An Unnecessary Evil

Towards the end of the millennium, we seemed to be witnessing many acts of reconciliation for past wrongs. In the last decade, more information about the assassination of John Kennedy has come to light. The family of Dr. Martin Luther King asked the justice department to reopen the investigation on the slain Civil Rights leader's death. Medgar Evers' killer was finally convicted, and sentenced after more than twenty-five years. Also about seventeen years ago, one of the men convicted of killing Malcolm X was given the opportunity to take a polygraph test, via live television, which he passed.

In 1965, Malcolm X's murder was suspected of being carried out by Black Muslims. These so-called Black Muslims were allegedly taught by the Nation of Islam leadership to despise Malcolm. The leadership had accused Malcolm X of being a Judas, a hypocrite. Some even went as far as to depict Malcolm X with horns, with his head chopped off in the newspaper that he helped to create, "Muhammad Speaks." The motive in Malcolm X's murder seemed obvious at the time, a group of rogue Muslims decided to eliminate Malcolm, because they perceived him to be slinging mud at their leader, Elijah Muhammad. The mud that Malcolm was reported to be slinging were rumors about Elijah Muhammad's adulterous relationships with several of his secretaries. Years later, the rumors were proven to be true.

One can draw many parallels between Malcolm X's death, and the Hanafi massacre. A few of the ministers whom Malcolm X had suggested were converting the Nation of Islam into a criminal organization, were the same ministers whose names appeared in connection with the war waged against the Hanafis. James Shabazz, a sworn enemy of Malcolm X, was heard making inflammatory comments. He suggested that Hamass Khaalis should be dealt with permanently, after receiving Khaalis' letter at his Newark temple. Coincidentally, the men convicted of murdering Malcolm X came from the Newark temple. One of the articles depicting Malcolm X as a hypocrite in "Muhammad Speaks" came from none other than Jeremiah Shabazz.

Based on most of my sources of research, Jeremiah Shabazz seems probable of being a major player in the conspiracy to assassinate Hamaas Khaalis. Minister Shabazz was quoted as given the order to kill James Price, according to some Philadelphia sources. Sources revealed to me that minister Shabazz was fearful that James Price would reveal his name as the person who gave the order to kill the Hanafis. Price was scheduled to return to the grand jury in January 1975, he was murdered on December 29, 1974. Someone did not want Price to see the New Year for a lot of reasons. The source also revealed that it was likely that Price would have told the grand jury what he knew because he had reportedly had a falling out with minister Shabazz. The fall out allegedly had to so with the rumor that minister Shabazz was dating Price's wife while he was locked up for the robbery-murder of the junk dealer in the spring of 1973. This was supposed to be the reason that Price initially began to cooperate with the federal prosecutors. The motive for the murders of the Hanafis may have been different from the motive to kill Malcolm, but it seemed that some of the players were the same.

The motive for the Hanafi murders was fundamentally about philosophical differences of opinion on the practice of Islam. About a week after the murders, a few members of the Nation of Islam, from temple #2 in Chicago, decided to write articles in the editorial pages of "Muhammad Speaks." They were responding to Hamaas Khaalis' charge that the Black Muslims killed his family because of his letter.

One of the articles came from minister Yusuf Shah, Malcolm X's former assistant at temple #7, who later became his nemesis. Shah wrote, "The brother in Washington, Hamaas Khaalis, leader of the Hanafi sect, is none other than Ernest, a mental patient, who was in the Nation of Islam. Messenger Muhammad took him in, gave him money, food, clothing, a nice car, and took care of him and his family. Now, the devil white man has put him on television, to try to denounce the messenger and his followers." (Muhammad Speaks, February, 1973).

Another parallel between the murders of Malcom X, and the Hanafis is the language of contempt. In their denouncement of the so-called denouncers, members of the Nation of Islam portrayed both Malcolm X, and Hamaas Khaalis as mental patients. In late 1964, Malcolm X's brother who was also a minister in the Nation of Islam, was requested by the National Secretary John Ali, to read a statement at a news conference about the rift between the Nation of Islam and Malcolm. Malcolm's brother spoke about the mental illness of their mother, and added that the disease had also claimed his brother Malcolm. Cults often utilize the same manipulation of language. If you can make those who oppose you out to be mentally ill, then your argument and your subsequent actions against them become justifiable.

Another member of Chicago's temple #2 wrote to express his disdain for Hamaas Khaalis in the same article. A member, who only identified himself as Melvin 12X wrote, "Mr. Khaalis, even if you were too weak to follow Mr. Muhammad, and because of your weakness did not believe he was the messenger of Allah, couldn't you see from his works and the respect he received from around the world, that he had divinity unequaled and far surpassing any man on this earth? Mr. Khaalis, I noticed on television that you were flying the American flag outside of your home, and even wearing it on your body. You claim to believe in Allah, but I did not see the flag of Islam, which is the star and crescent, anywhere near your house, or on your person. Mr. Khaalis, you are making a fool of yourself. You cannot worship two gods at the same time" (Muhammad Speaks, February 1973).

About two years after the massacre, the messenger, Elijah Muhammad died at the age of seventy-seven. Elijah Muhammad's son Wallace Deen Muhammad, took over after his father's death. With full support of the ministers, Wallace Deen Muhammad became the leader of the Nation of Islam. He appointed Jeremiah Shabazz to become Eastern regional minister, head of all temples in the eastern cities. This meant that Jeremiah Shabazz would be working from the largest temple on the east coast, Temple #7. Many believed the elevation of Jeremiah Shabazz to this newly made position was Minister Muhammad's way of "cleaning house."

Minister Muhammad had sided with Malcolm X during the feud between Malcolm X and the ministers in the Nation of Islam, and because of his loyalty to Malcolm against his father, Wallace was suspended for over a year. After his reinstatement into the Nation, it was said that Wallace was disgusted by all the headlines of criminal activity, from those professing to be Muslims, in cities like Philadelphia. He was also aware of minister Louis Farrakhan's desire to lead the organization, upon hearing of the messenger's death. So when Minister Muhammad elevated Jeremiah Shabazz's position, thus moving him out of Philadelphia to New York, he also moved minister Farrakhan, who was in New York to Chicago, reportedly to keep an eye on him. A month after minister Muhammad's shuffle of his most threatening ministers, he gave a speech that shocked America.

Minister Muhammad spoke to a crowd of one hundred thousand at Madison Square Garden, in the summer of 1975. He declared that from now and forever, mosques, as they were now called, would be open to whites. In that once sentence, minister Muhammad made a break from his father's "white devil" separatist philosophy.

On January 18, 1976, three years after the Hanafi massacre, and a year before the Hanafi siege on Washington, minister Muhammad made more changes that helped to shift the philosophy of the Nation of Islam closer toward the mainstream. He announced plans to launch a nationwide voter registration drive. The rationale was to give Muslims more of an active role in politics. Previously, most Muslims avoided what they referred to as "white man's politics." It seemed that minister Muhammad's politics were parallel to that of the late minister Malcolm X. Prior to his death, Malcolm had also launched a voter registration drive through his organization; Muslim Mosque Inc. The third charge made by minister Muhammad renamed the New York mosque where Malcolm preached, Malcolm X mosque. In doing so, minister Muhammad was sending a message that the spiritual and philosophical feud was over.

Even with all the changes made, the Nation of Islam continued to feel the heat connected to the Hanafi massacre, as well as from activities of the Black Mafia in Philadelphia. Simultaneously, the Philadelphia office of the F.B.I. was preparing to indict twenty members of the Black Mafia on heroin trafficking. Most of those indicted were also members of Temple #12. A former security guard for minister Muhammad stated that the ministers had given Muslims the order to murder seven people. So after conducting his internal inquiry into the incident, minister Muhammad decided to make another change.

In February 1976, minister Muhammad stripped Jeremiah Shabazz of all of his titles and duties. After serving twenty-two years in the Nation of Islam, Jeremiah Shabazz was once again a rank and file member. About a week later, Jeremiah Shabazz gave an interview with a newspaper reporter. He stated that he was resigning his post as a minister in the Nation of Islam. After leaving his post, Jeremiah took a job as an administrative assistant for heavyweight boxing champion, Muhammad Ali.

A few years after minister Muhammad's "house cleaning," the mosque became masjids, and the ministers became Imams. Some of the membership of the old Nation of Islam left to join minister Louis Farrakhan, who felt that the changes being made were not in the interest of Black people. Others left with another minister named Silas Muhammad, who had the same idea, but most stayed and became Sunni Muslims with Imam Warith Deen Muhammad. The Hanafis were also Sunni Muslims.

Imam Muhammad's group was renamed the World Community of Islam in the West (W.C.I.W.), in 1977, the same year of the Hanafi siege on Washington. Most of the members of Elijah Muhammad's Nation of Islam, referred to as the first resurrection, were more comfortable following the messenger's son than either Louis Farrakhan or Silas Muhammad.

Ten years after the Hanafi murders, and six years after the siege on Washington, no one could tell the difference between the Hanafi's practice of Islam, and those practicing in the American Muslim Mission, under Imam Muhammad's leadership. The Imam had totally transformed his father's organization, from a white people excluding, separatist movement, to a mainstream Islamic fellowship, embracing all people. Imam Muhammad had also conducted a sweep of corrupt Muslim officials, and replaced them with Arabic speaking, Qur'an-educated Muslims. Most of the Muslims who were staunch supporters of the old Nation of Islam transitioned with Imam Muhammad.

Even those imprisoned, who killed because they thought the messenger was being disrespected, acquiesced and became Sunni Muslims. Most of the prisoners, including my father, who are spending life in prison, realized that they were duped. They were duped by leaders, whom they thought were loyal to the struggle for their independence, as defined by Elijah Muhammad. They went to jail for those leaders and the messenger. When they were convicted, the leadership called them "bad apples," and "nonbelievers." They discovered that the undying loyalty between themselves and the Nation of Islam was one-sided.

Almost twenty years after the Hanafi massacre, Imam Muhammad led the prayer that began the 104th session of the U.S. Congress. I wondered what brother Melvin 12X thought about Imam Muhammad leading Congress into prayer, after writing his contemptuous letter about Hamaas Khaalis' display of the American flag. Now over thirty years after the assassination of Malcolm X, and over a quarter of a century after the deaths of the seven Hanafis, one would have to be an expert in Islam to explain any spiritual/philosophical differences between Hamaas Khaalis' Hanafi Muslims, and the Sunni Muslims practicing under the leadership of Imam Muhammad.

As adults, we realize that death is necessary. The old make room for the young. However, the fashion and time of death, like the babies and young adults who were murdered in

Washington, were absolutely unnecessary. It wasn't even a matter of irreconcilable differences, as we have witnessed the fusion of the two groups' philosophical polarities. Perhaps the added ingredient of law enforcement facilitated a deeper misunderstanding, which fed the aggression from one side. Whatever the case, those misunderstandings sealed the fates of those occupying the Khaalis residence on January 18, 1973. A goal of mine in writing this story is to officially record the story of this tragic event so that it would not be acted out on another family ever again, at least not from lack of knowing.

Chronology

1923

Legislation is introduced to reduce the importation of opium for the manufacturing of heroin.

1933

W.D. Fard gives Elijah Poole the teachings of Islam. Elijah Poole converts from Christianity to Islam and changes his name from Elijah Poole to Elijah Muhammad. Fard and Muhammad open a Muslim temple in Detroit, Michigan. Fard mysteriously disappears.

Elijah Muhammad opens second Muslim temple in Chicago, Illinois.

1946

Major Coxson successfully runs for senior class president. Jeremiah Pugh is Major Coxson's rival classmate. Jeremiah Pugh later changes his name to Jeremia Shabazz.

1954-1968

The Modern Civil Rights Movement

1954

Temple #12 is established by Jeremiah Shabazz and Malcolm X.

1956

Congress declares that heroin is now banned.

1959

Elijah Muhammad sends Jeremiah Shabazz to Atlanta to spread Islam throughout the south. Jeremiah Shabazz becomes top official of southern temples and a part of Elijah Muhammad's inner circle becomes top official of southern temples and a part of Elijah Muhammad's inner circle.

1950s-1960s

Major Coxson is arrested many times for gambling and con schemes. By mid 1960's Major Coxson, aka Maje, is considered a legend in the criminal community of Philadelphia.

February, 1964

Muhammad Ali announces that he is a member of the Nation of Islam.

1965

Malcolm X accuses members of the Nation of Islam of fire bombing his house by the orders of Elijah Muhammad.

February 21, 1965

Malcolm X is assassinated.

January, 1969

Charles Ben Ami is held up, robbed, and shot to death at his gas station in West Oak Lane, Philadelphia. (47)

Nineteen year old James Price and three of his friends are charged with the murder of Charles Ben Ami, a forty-five year old Czechoslovakian man who had moved to Philadelphia. This case is highly publicized and the Jewish community was enraged.

1971

Lew Alcindor, later known as Kareem Abdul Jabbar, a basketball player for the Milwaukee Bucks, purchases the house on 7700 16ᵃ Street, NW Washington D.C. Kareem Abdul Jabbar donated $78,000 home to Imam Khaliffa Hamaas Abdul Khaalis.

1972

Major Coxson begins his campaign for Mayor of Camden, New Jersey.

Jeremiah Shabazz returns to Philadelphia

December1972

The rift between practitioners of Sunni Islam and the Nation of Islam grows deeper after Malcolm X's assassination and comes to a fever pitch. Khaalifa Hamaas Abdul Khaalis sends letters to the ministers of seventy-seven "Black Muslim" temples.

January 17, 1973

9:30 p.m. Two cars full with young black men pull up to a downtown motel at 501 New York Avenue, located in the northeast section of Washington. Seven men check into rooms 27 and 29

10:15 p.m.

Four men from room 29 join their friends in room 27 for a meeting.

10:45 p.m

Four men drive to the northwest section of Washington to take a look at the exits while the three remaining wait at the motel.

11:00 p.m.

A caller from out of town phones the motel. Their call is transferred to room 27.

11:45 p.m.

All four men return and retire to their rooms.

January 18, 1973

The Khaalis family is massacred.

4:45 p.m.

The police arrive at the Khaalis property.

January 22, 1973

The ballistic report confirms that the weapons found outside the Khaalis home are the weapons that were used the murder the Khaalis family. A partial print is found on one of the weapons. No matches to the print are found in Washington. Report is sent out to Baltimore, New York, and Philadelphia. Partial print is matched with a known felon in Philadelphia.

6:00 p.m.

Mr. Khaalis gives a press conference in his living room. Print, media, and radio stations attend for Mr. Khaalis' first public remarks about the loss of his family.

February 8, 1973

Ernest Kelly is visited by four impeccably well-dressed young men with guns. The leader of the four, John Clark, escorts Ernest to the bank to withdraw $100,000, while the other three men hold his wife, children, and grandchildren hostage at their home. William Christian, Richard Dabney, and John Griffin are the other men.

February 12, 1973

Theodore Moody is held at Philadelphia Detention Center.

March 1973

The Philadelphia Yellow Cab Company (the city's largest taxi service) is robbed in a hold up. The two robbers get away with $52,000.

The next day

Jerome Sinclair gives a bail bondsman $42,000, 10% required to release the four kidnapping suspects of Ernest Kelly's family.

March 16 1973

John Clark is picked up by the FBI and charged with robbery and kidnapping.

April 5, 1973

Three men rob and hold up the Baldwin Frankford Dairies office in Northeast Philadelphia. They leave with cash & credit cards from employees and $5,00 from the office safe.

April 8, 1973

James Price sits in an interrogation room at the Philadelphia Police Department Headquarters for the murder of Myers Abrams.

April 25, 1973

Sarah Robinson, a 40 year old motel chambermaid, is informed that she is needed to appear at a lineup on May 3ʳᵈ to identify some of the eight men who stayed at the motel on January 17ᵗʰ.

11:00 a.m.

Detectives Branson and Jacobs go to Philadelphia to gather subpoenas.

May 1973

Major Coxson unsuccessfully runs for Mayor of Camden, New Jersey.

June 8, 1973

4:00 a.m. Major Coxson hears a knock on his door. Four gunmen force their way in. Major Coxson is shot, as well as his wife Lois, and two children, Lita and Toro. Major Coxson and Lita are killed. (50)

June 9, 1973

Two homicide detectives arrive in Cherry Hill, New Jersey at the scene of Major Coxson's and his step-daughter's murders.

July, 1973

James Price testifies to a grand jury about his and others' roles in the Hanafi murders.

August 15, 1973

Grand jury indicts John Clark, William Christian, John Griffin, Ronald Harvey, Theodore Moody, James Price, Jerome Sinclair, and Thomas Clinton in the Hanafi murder trial.

August 17, 1973

Ronald Harvey fails to appear to court after being out on bail.

August 28, 1973

Extradition hearing is held for the four in custody.

September 4, 1973

John Clark, Theodore Moody, James Price, and Jerome Sinclair attend their arraignment hearing.

The FBI added Ronald Harvey, to the FBI'S top ten most wanted.

Two FBI agents are given the task to locate fugitives through "street surveillance," i.e.
informants.

September 6, 1973

FBI agents begin wiretapping John Griffin's and William Christian's family members' phones.

September 30, 1973

FBI agents hear Richard Dabney complaining on the phone to a woman about money he owed to John 43X. Pancer and Smallwood identify John 43X as John Griffin. Agent Parker and Smallwood visit Dabney.

October 3, 1973

FBI agents capture John Griffin and William Christian in an apartment in Jacksonville, Florida where Griffin and Christian had been staying since May with their wives and children.

October 5, 1973

John Griffin and William Christian are extradited to Washington, D.C. for the Hanafi killings.

February 6, 1974

Defendants are tried.

March 25, 1974

Radio broadcast airs a message from the Nation of Islam, by Louis Farrakhan, leader of Temple #7 in Harlem. This is considered a veiled threat to James Price.

March 26, 1974

Judge Braman receives a note from Price's attorney.

October, 1974

Ronald Harvey's trial begins.

November 20, 1974

Ronald Harvey receives a guilty verdict from the jury.

December 29, 1974

8:00 a.m. Calvin, an inmate staying on D Block for isolation, hears James Price being murdered.

January, 1975

Ronald Harvey is sent to New Jersey to stand for the murders of Major Coxson and his stepdaughter.

January 20, 1975

District Court of Appeals grants John Griffin a new trial.

Summer, 1975

Wallace Deen Muhammad (son of Elijah Muhammad) makes a speech at Madison Square Garden and states that mosques will now be open to whites.

January 18, 1976

Minister Muhammad makes changes to the Nation of Islam philosophy that shift it more towards mainstream. He plans to launch a nationwide voter registration drive.

February, 1976

Minister Muhammad strips minister Shabazz of all his titles and duties. Jeremiah Shabazz takes a job as Muhammad Ali's administrative assistant.

February 8, 1976

John Griffin Jr. and his family enter the Witness Protection Program.

October 5, 1976

Amina Khaalis testifies for the prosecution about   John Griffin's role in the murders.

October 9, 1976

Ms. Khaalis' physician testifies in court that she is not able to attend the trial.

October 13, 1976

Judge Braman rules that Ms. Khaalis will not have to come back to court for cross-examination.

March 9, 1977

11:00 a.m. Four men attack the National Headquarters B'nai B'rith. Sixty-five hostages are taken.

12:00 p.m. Two men invade Washington's Islamic Center

2:40 p.m.

The District Building in Washington D.C. is invaded. Khalifa Hamaas Abdul Khaalis states that he is waging war.

3:30 p.m.

Khalifa Hamaas Abdul Khaalis addresses reporters outside that the Hanafi Muslims are waging war. This lasts three hours.

March 11, 1977

Khaalis releases hostages and agrees to conditions. The 12 men responsible are arraigned.

May 31, 1977

Trial is held for Hanafi siege. Hamaas Khaalis and 11 co-defendants stand trial.

July 24, 1977

Jury finds Hamaas Khaalis and co-defendants guilty.

August, 1977

John's family goes back into the witness protection.

October 11, 1977

John Griffin's third trial begins.

November, 1977

John Griffin Sr. is acquitted in the Hanafi murders after three trials.

BIBLIOGRAPHY

BOOKS

Bennet, William. *The Book of Virtues: A Treasury of Great Moral Stories.* Simon & Schuster, 1997.

Haley, Alex. *Autobiography of Malcolm X.* Ballantine Books, 1992.

Lomax, Louis. *When the Word is Given: A Report on Elijah Muhammad, Malcolm X, and the Black Muslim World.* Greenwood Publishing Group, 1979.

NEWSPAPER ARTICLES

Muhammad Speaks, Temple University Archive Department

Philadelphia Daily News, Temple University Archive Department

Philadelphia Inquirer, Temple University Archive Department

The New York Times, Temple University Archive Department

The Washington Post, Temple University Archive Department

www.ingramcontent.com/pod-product-compliance
Lightning Source LLC
Chambersburg PA
CBHW020915090426
42736CB00008B/645